First Published by Padblocks Ltd 2009
©2009 Erika Parry

Padblocks Ltd
Fishponds Road
Wokingham
Berkshire
RG41 2QX
www.padblocks.com

Written and Illustrated by Erika Parry
Designed by Deborah Tait
Compiled by Leigh Taberer
Printed in China

ISBN 978-0-9561981-0-5

All rights reserved. No part of this publication may be reproduced, stored in a retrieval system, or transmitted in any form or by any means electronic, mechanical, photocopying, recording or otherwise, without written permission of the publishers.

TASTE THE FLAVOURS SOW THE SEEDS

Inspirational recipes from a small garden

Written and Illustrated by
Erika Parry

Padblocks Ltd 2009

CONTENTS

1) Preface

2) Apples and Pears

3) Green Beans

4) Blueberry/ Bilberry

5) Courgettes

6) Lavender

7) Mint

8) Peas

9) Raspberries

10) Roses

11) Salad Leaves

12) Spinach and Chard

13) Strawberries

14) Tarragon

15) Tomatoes

16) Violets

PREFACE

It is wonderful to grow your own food, especially those items which are difficult to find, and garden centres supply all you require in the way of seeds, seedlings and plants.

I have created recipes which I personally like and are tasted and approved by my friends and family. I am trying to express my personality through food and design, and my choices of different fruit, flowers, vegetables and herbs, most of which can be grown in pots and window boxes for the small garden or flat.

They are different, fun and not too difficult to cook... I hope they will inspire you to try something new. There are so many excellent garden centres to be found and so many marvellous ingredients to encourage the enthusiastic cook

Erika

∗ Thank you to my wonderful husband Croose, without whose help, patience, taste-buds and understanding this book would not have been created!!

APPLES and PEARS

' LIKE THE SWEET APPLE WHICH REDDENS
UPON THE TOPMOST BOUGH.'
Dante Gabriel Rossetti 1823-1882

Apple and Parsnip Soup (Serves 6)

900g/2lbs parsnips, peeled and cut into chunks
1 onion peeled and chopped
2-3 Bramley apples, peeled, cored and chopped
Salt and 1$^1/_2$ dessertspoons curry powder
850ml/1$^1/_2$ pints chicken stock
150ml/ $^1/_4$ pint double cream to 'swirl'

- Put parsnips, onion, and apples in a large saucepan together with the stock and a little water and salt.
- Simmer until soft.
- Add curry powder and liquidise, adding more if liked.
- Serve with hot rolls and a swirl of double cream. Good hot or cold and lovely in winter.

APPLES HAVE SUCH A LOVELY FRESH TASTE. PURÉED APPLE IS ONE OF THE BEST FOODS TO GIVE TO PEOPLE WHO ARE UNWELL.

Apple and Herring (Serves 3-4)

4 dill or red wine sweet cure Herring (chopped)
2 Granny Smith apples, cored and chopped
3 small cooked beetroot, chopped
1 finely sliced small red onion
2 hard boiled eggs
Crème fraiche or sour cream
Ground black pepper
Dill, chopped

Combine everything and arrange on salad leaves.
Sprinkle with dill and chopped eggs.

Apple Sauce with Quinces

- Peel 2 quinces, 3 Bramley apples, 2 Granny Smith apples.
- Core and chop apples and simmer with water to cover and 75g/3oz golden granulated sugar. Add quinces.
- After 10 minutes remove quinces, cut in half, remove core and dice.
- Put back with apples and simmer until soft but keep some pieces of apple and quince intact.
- Serve cold with pork chops or roast pork or suckling pig, with new potatoes and a green salad.

My Chicken Normande (Serves 4-6)

4-6 skinned chicken breasts
75g/3oz pancetta cubes
2 shallots peeled and finely diced
4 Cox apples, peeled, cored and neatly sliced
Salt, ground black pepper
Butter and corn oil for frying
2-3 tablespoons Calvados
300ml/ 1/2 pint double cream

- Cut the chicken into small neat strips and pat dry with kitchen paper.
- Fry the apple slices in butter, turning often until golden, and set aside. In a separate pan, using oil, fry the shallots until golden.
- Add the chicken pieces and pancetta, turning frequently.
- Flambé with Calvados adding seasoning and cream and combine the apples with the chicken.
- Allow the cream to bubble for a few minutes.
- Serve with rosti potatoes or boiled rice.

Caramel Pears (Serves 4-6)

700g/1½ lbs pears (William or Conference)
50g/2oz butter
75g/3oz sugar
300ml/½ pint double cream

- Peel, core and neatly slice pears.
- Heat butter in a frying pan and when nut brown, add pears turning frequently.
- Sprinkle with the sugar and allow to caramelize.
- Immediately add the cream, simmering for a few minutes to allow the caramel to dissolve. Serve warm with vanilla ice-cream.

The same recipe can substitute apples (Cox, Granny Smith) for pears.

Apple Puree with Vanilla

Cook Bramley apples, sugar (equal quantities to peeled apples) and a little water and 2 vanilla pods gently until soft. Remove pods, rinse under tap and split in half, scraping out seeds into the apple mixture. Cook carefully not allowing it to stick to the bottom of the pan. When nearly cooked (treat as for jam) add 3 teaspoons of pure vanilla essence.
Put in a hot, attractive jar.

William Pear stuffed with Marzipan (Serves 6-8)

6 William pears
50g/2 oz golden granulated sugar
Water to cover
2 teaspoons vanilla essence
1 egg white
75g/3oz ground almonds
50g/2oz caster sugar
75g/3oz flaked almonds
175g/6oz plain chocolate
300ml / 1/2 pint double cream
1 tablespoon sugar
1 dessertspoon unsalted butter

- Peel the pears and drop into simmering sugar, water and vanilla essence. When they become transparent remove from heat and leave to cool.
- Cut in half and remove core carefully with a teaspoon.
- Mix the sugar and ground almonds and bind with a little slightly beaten egg white.
- Spoon into the pear halves.
- Dry fry the almond flakes until golden and spike into the marzipan following the shape of the pear.
- Melt the butter, sugar and cream in a double boiler or a bowl over simmering water – add the broken chocolate and cool.
- Spoon onto a plate in a circle shape and put a pear half in the centre.

William Pear and Almond Crumble (Serves 4)

900g/2lbs pears peeled and cored
1 tablespoon golden granulated sugar
110g/4oz butter
2 tablespoons dried skimmed milk powder
3 tablespoons ground almonds
175g/6oz plain flour
1 tablespoon flaked almonds

- Grease an ovenproof dish and set the oven to 300F/150C/Gas Mark 2.
- Slice the pears neatly and put in the dish.
- Make a crumble mixture by rubbing the butter and flour between the fingers until it looks like bread crumbs.
- Add a little sugar, followed by ground almonds and milk powder.
- Spoon over the pears.
- Sprinkle with golden granulated sugar, and when nearly cooked, scatter flaked almonds over the top.
Serve lukewarm with double cream.

THIS IS VERY SUBTLE AND DELICATE.

Almond Blossom

Erika's Fantastic William Pear Trifle (Serves 6-8)

- Gently poach 900g/2lbs William pears which have been peeled, cored and cut into four. Use very little water, 2 tablespoons caster sugar and half a vanilla pod.
- Keep the slices whole, so low heat - they should look transparent when ready. Set aside to cool.
- Using a pretty glass bowl, put in a packet of trifle sponges cut to fit the bottom of the bowl.
- With a slotted spoon, remove the pears from the liquid and layer them carefully over the sponge cake, rounded sides uppermost.
- Mix together 2 tablespoons pear cooking liquid together with 2 tablespoons Eau de Vie de Poire William (obtainable at specialist wine shops or Selfridges and Harrods).
- Cover with 110g/4oz ground almonds.
- Mask with a good custard made with egg, cream and vanilla *see 'Raspberry Jelly with Creamy Custard'.
- Spoon softly whipped double cream over the surface and decorate with toasted flaked almonds.
- At the last minute decorate with Ratafia or Amaretti biscuits.

THIS IS A WONDERFUL DESSERT SUITABLE FOR THE VERY BEST FEASTS! IT GETS THE FAMILY VOTE EVERY TIME I ASK 'WHAT SHALL I GIVE THEM FOR PUD?' THE ONLY TIME I DECLINE IS WHEN I RUN OUT OF EAU DE VIE DE POIRE WILLIAM, WHICH IS VERY SPECIAL!

Erika's Harvest Apple Trifle (Serves 6-8)

This is a suitable 'pud' for the time of Harvest Festival. It can be made in large quantities and served in rustic bowls or mixing bowls.

- Cook 900g/2lbs peeled, cored and sliced Granny Smith apples with very little liquid, juice of 1 lemon and sugar to taste.
- Try and keep the slices whole, so low heat.
- Set aside to cool.
- In the bottom of a dish put cubes of sponge cake or trifle sponge. Sprinkle with medium sherry and cover with the cold apple.
- Cover with 110g/4oz ground almonds.
- Mask with a good custard made with eggs, cream and vanilla.
- Spoon softly whipped double cream over the surface and decorate with
- Ratafia or Amaretti biscuits and flaked almonds.
  Instead of cream a lovely alternative is Cider Syllabub

Cider Syllabub

In a bowl mix 300ml/ 1/2 pint dry cider, 2 tablespoons brandy, juice and grated rind of 1 lemon, 75g/3oz caster sugar. Leave to stand for several hours for the flavours to mix and the sugar to dissolve. Pour 300ml/ 1/2 pint double cream slowly onto cider mixture stirring gently. Whisk until soft peaks are obtained. Spoon the syllabub over the trifle and decorate.

FINE GREEN BEANS

Green Bean (Starter or Salad)   (Serves 4)

800g/1½ lbs fine green beans
2 lemons
Bunch of radishes (optional)
Extra virgin olive oil
Sea salt, freshly ground pepper

- Top and tail beans and steam for 5-7 minutes, no lid.
- Refresh in iced water.
- Put on plates with a halved lemon, salt and pepper and olive oil to serve. Coarsely grated radish is a colourful addition.

Green Bean and Pancetta Bundles

- Steam and refresh fine trimmed green beans.
- Make little bunches and wrap with slices of pancetta, holding if necessary with a wooden cocktail stick.
- Grill, turning several times.
- Remove cocktail sticks. This provides an elegant bundle of beans to accompany steak, duck, etc.

Green Bean Salsa

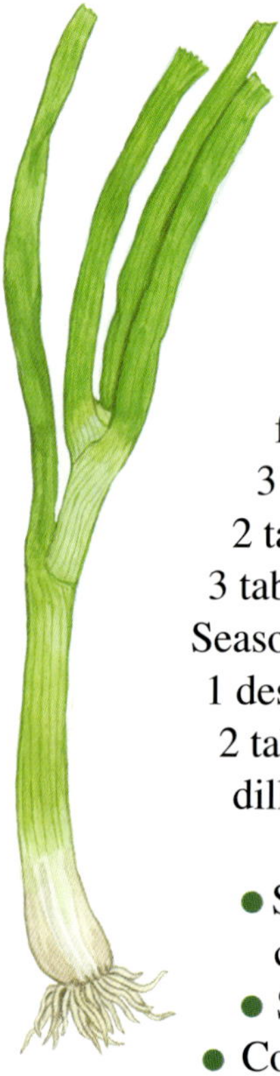

450g/1lb fine green beans (trimmed)
450g/1lb shelled broad beans
1 de-seeded and diced green pepper
Half a cucumber, diced
1 clove of garlic, crushed
Half a green chilli, de-seeded and finely chopped
3 spring onions, chopped
2 tablespoons white wine vinegar
3 tablespoons olive oil
Seasoning
1 dessertspoon maple syrup, or sugar
2 tablespoons of either chopped basil, dill, parsley or mint

- Steam the beans and refresh in cold water and cut into 1 inch lengths.
- Steam broad beans and refresh.
- Combine all the ingredients.
- If serving with fish, add dill.

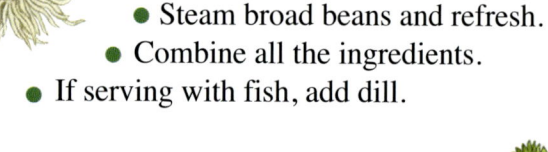

Beans, Bacon, Pear and Potato (Serves 6)

This is simple and delicious and a good family meal. Quantities need not be strictly accurate.

900g/2lbs fine green beans, runner beans or bobby beans
300g/10 1/2 oz back bacon, dry cured or maple cured
450g/1lb pears (Conference or William)
450g/1lb potatoes, thickly sliced
Salt and freshly ground black pepper

- In a large saucepan put a layer of mixed beans, followed by bacon and then more beans.
- Sprinkle with seasoning.
- Carefully add a layer of sliced potatoes followed with a top layer of sliced pears.
- Add water to cover and simmer until cooked, making sure potatoes retain their shape (30-40 minutes).
The broth makes a lovely soup if there is any left over!
It also reheats well for another meal.

The recipe comes from German farmers who kept their pig, grew their beans and potatoes and had orchards of pears.

Salad Niçoise (Serves 6-8)

New potatoes (cooked)
Fine green beans (cooked and refreshed)
Green peppers
Lettuce heart
Tomatoes
Tinned tuna in oil, or grilled fresh tuna
Hardboiled eggs
Tinned anchovies
Olive oil
Red wine vinegar
Seasoning
Chives.

- Use a large bowl and line with lettuce heart and cover with slices of cooked new potatoes.
- Add a layer of sliced (de-seeded) green pepper, followed by sliced rounds of tomato and seasoning.
- Cover with flaked tuna (2-3 tins).
- Slice hardboiled eggs and cover the circumference of the bowl (about 8 eggs).
- Make a criss-cross pattern with anchovies placing black olives artistically in between.
- Pour olive oil carefully allowing it to run down sides of bowl.
- Drizzle red wine vinegar over and decorate with snipped chives.

This is a really good dish and was how I made it in France. Impossible to give exact quantities – depends on how many people and how big the dish.

Green Bean Banquet (Serves 4)

This is a surprisingly good and tasty dish and is a fantastic supper topped with a fried egg.

450g/1lb fine green beans
6 medium tomatoes (cut into 4)
1 large onion (cut in half and finely sliced)
1 large garlic clove (finely chopped)
1-2 inches fresh ginger (finely chopped)
2-3 medium potatoes (peeled and diced)
1/2 teaspoon of curry powder
1/2 teaspoon of turmeric powder
1 teaspoon salt
200ml/7 fl oz boiling water
A squeeze of tomato paste

- Trim the beans and cut in half.
- Heat 2 tablespoons olive oil in a large saucepan and gently fry the onions, followed by the garlic and ginger for 1 minute.
- Stir in the spices and salt, followed by the tomatoes and boiling water.
- Bubble away for 5 minutes then add the beans, potatoes and tomato puree.
- Cook until beans are tender and the potatoes intact but cooked. Serve with chopped mint or coriander.

THIS DISH IS SERVED THROUGHOUT THE MIDDLE EAST WITH RICE OR BREAD, BUT NO POTATOES. OKRA CAN BE SUBSTITUTED FOR BEANS. DO NOT BE TEMPTED TO USE MORE SPICE - THE FLAVOURS ARE PERFECT AND WITH THE ADDITION OF POTATOES ALL THE VEGETABLES ARE COOKED TOGETHER. MAKE SURE MOST OF THE LIQUID HAS EVAPORATED.

Fricasse of Mixed Beans with Almonds

200g /7oz runner beans (cut on slant)
200g /7oz fine green beans (trimmed)
200g /7oz sugar snap peas (trimmed)
100g /3 1/2 oz podded peas
100g /3 1/2 oz podded broad beans
2 finely chopped shallots
Butter
Seasoning
Crème fraiche
Vegetable Stock
Toasted flaked almonds (optional)

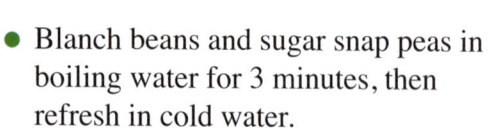

- Blanch beans and sugar snap peas in boiling water for 3 minutes, then refresh in cold water.
- Sweat the shallots in butter for a few minutes to soften, not colour.
- Add the remainder of the vegetables together with 300ml/10fl oz/ 1/2 pint vegetable stock and seasoning.
- Simmer gently until tender.
- Mix 2 teaspoons cornflour with a tablespoon of water and add to the mixture stirring well to thicken.
- Add 2 tablespoons crème fraiche and chopped herbs such as flat leaf parsley.
  *For an extra special touch, scatter with toasted flaked almonds.

Green Green Soup

1 onion (chopped)
1 clove of garlic (chopped)
2 potatoes (peeled and chopped)
1 small cucumber (chopped)
1-2 bunches watercress
175g/6oz fresh or frozen shelled peas
175g/6oz fine green beans (cut in 3)
700ml/1¼ pints chicken or vegetable stock
Finely chopped chives or flat leaf parsley

- Fry onion and garlic lightly in olive oil.
- Add potatoes and stock and simmer until tender.
- Add peas and cucumber and continue cooking, adding the watercress for a few minutes at the end.
- Season with salt and pepper and if liked, juice of half a lemon.
- Liquidise the soup.
- Steam the fine green beans and combine with the soup, adding a knob of butter.
- Serve with finely snipped chives and chopped flat leaf parsley. A slice of grilled bruschetta with grilled mozzarella goes well with this soup.

Note: This is a healthy tasting soup and stands up well without butter.

THE VERSATILE FRENCH GREEN BEAN IS ONE OF THE NICEST OF GARDEN VEGETABLES AND ALTHOUGH CALLED 'FRENCH' IT ORIGINATED IN PERU!!

Green Beans and Flageolets

The perfect accompaniment to roast lamb.

700g/1 1/2 lbs fine green beans (trimmed)
2-3 tins of flageolet beans
Freshly ground black pepper
1 carton crème fraiche
2 cloves of garlic

- Steam the beans (no lid) and refresh in cold water.
- Drain the flageolets.
- Fry chopped garlic in olive oil.
- Place all in a large pan or wok together with several spoonfuls of crème fraiche and seasoning.
- Gently heat through.

Potatoes are unnecessary – as the flageolets are starchy.

GARDENING TIPS FOR GREEN BEANS

Can be grown in large pots or a wigwam in good compost.
They crop 8 weeks after planting.
The more they are picked, the more they produce.

BLUEBERRY OR BILBERRY

'Strange to see how a good dinner and
feasting reconciles everybody.'

Samuel Pepys 1665

Lamb Chops or Noisettes with Blueberries
Serves 4

2 chump chops or 4 noisettes of lamb
2 shallots, peeled and finely chopped
2 tablespoons small blueberries or bilberries
2 tablespoons double cream
Salt, freshly milled black pepper
1 tablespoon thyme leaves

Ask the butcher to cut the chops lengthways and to remove the bone. It makes them slim and browns the fat nicely.
- Fry the shallots until nearly brown in 1 tablespoon olive oil. Push to one side in the frying pan.
- Add the chops or noisettes until brown on both sides.
- Add salt and pepper and put on dinner plates.
- Put the blueberries in the pan stirring until some juices start to show. Add the cream and allow to bubble.
- Spoon the blueberry cream sauce over the lamb.
I serve this dish with little rosti shapes using metal rings.

Blueberry and Maple Cheesecake (Baked)

Biscuit Base
125g/4 1/2 oz wholemeal digestive biscuits
50g/2oz pecan nuts
75g/3oz butter, melted

Filling
250g/9oz curd cheese
250g/9oz cream cheese
25g/1oz caster sugar
2 eggs
150ml/5fl oz/ 1/4 pint maple syrup
1 tablespoon plain flour
300g/10 1/2 oz blueberries

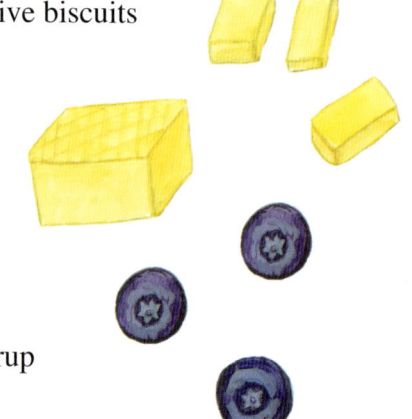

- Butter a 21cm loose bottom, spring form cake tin and line base with baking parchment including a narrow strip for the sides.
- Crush the digestive biscuits in a paper bag with a rolling pin or blitz with a food processor.
- Chop pecan nuts finely and mix crumbs and nuts with butter.
- Spread over the cake base and work slightly up the sides.
- Chill in the fridge for 3/4 hr.
- Set the oven to 180C/350F/Gas 4
- In a large mixing bowl, combine the curd and cream cheeses.
- Mix the caster sugar and maple syrup, beating well.
- Add the eggs, one at a time, beating well.
- In a small bowl, tip the blueberries and flour, shaking so they are coated in flour.
- Pour the maple mixture into the cake tin and scatter the blueberries over the top.
- Bake for 35 - 40 minutes then turn oven off and leave door open.
- When cheesecake is cold, cover and leave overnight in fridge.
- Remove from tin, peeling paper from the sides and brush surface with maple syrup using a pastry brush.

Blueberry Sauce to serve with Game

- Cook a small punnet of blueberries with 1 chopped shallot, a clove of chopped garlic, chicken stock, 1 glass red wine, 1 tablespoon balsamic vinegar, salt, coarsely ground black pepper and 1 tablespoon redcurrant jelly.
- When blueberries are soft, reserve a few for decoration and liquidise the rest.
- Thicken if desired with 1 teaspoon cornflour mixed with water and quickly stirred into the sauce.
- Before serving stir in several cubes of butter - this will make the sauce glossy.

Serve with pheasant, partridge, venison, or duck.

Blueberry Tips

- Use lemon or lime juice to bring out the flavour of blueberries
- Maple syrup and cream is very good with blueberries and is served like this in Canada and America.
- They are a welcome addition to any recipe calling for 'mixed berries'.
- Less sugar is required for making jam – 225g/8oz sugar to 450g/1lb blueberries.
- Jam can be eaten with clotted cream.
- Can be dried in a cool oven, stored in glass jars, and used instead of currants.

BLUEBERRIES MAKE ONE THINK OF THE GREAT OUTDOORS AND WILD THINGS. THEIR HABITAT IS HEATHS, MOORS, FORESTS AND OPEN SPACES.
WHEN IN NORWAY THE BLUEBERRIES WERE VERY PROLIFIC AND ONE WOULD SCRAPE THEM OFF THE BUSHES WITH A SPECIAL COMB AND BLOW THE LEAVES AWAY. THE NORTH AMERICAN BLUEBERRY IS BIGGER AND IS CULTIVATED. A VERY GOOD PURPLE DYE IS MADE FROM THE JUICE.
ACCORDING TO WILLIAM COLES IN 1657 THE JUICE 'GIVETH A PURPLISH COLOUR TO THE HANDS AND LIPS OF THEM THAT HANDLE AND EAT THEM.'

Blueberry Frangipane Slice
Serves 6

- Cover swiss roll tins with baking parchment and set the oven to 200C/400F/Gas 6.
- Lay puff pastry sheets on the baking paper and roll the sides and ends giving a little thickness. Prick with a fork and put in the oven for 15-20 mins.
- Remove and cool.
- Using electric beaters combine 150g/5 1/2 oz soft butter with 300g/10oz caster sugar. Beat until fluffy and add 3 beaten eggs gradually. Fold in 2 tablespoons plain flour and 125g/4 1/2 oz ground almonds and 1 tablespoon Kirsch.
- Spoon onto the pastry and carefully place blueberries on top.
- Bake for about 25 minutes until golden and set. Leave in the tin for a few minutes and cut into squares or slices.
- Serve sprinkled with glucose or icing sugar.
  Vanilla ice-cream, clotted cream or mascarpone compliment this dessert very well.

Erika's Blueberry and Lime Syllabub
Serves 6

4 1/2 tablespoons white wine
1 tablespoon sherry
Juice of half a lime
1 1/2 tablespoons caster sugar
300ml/10fl oz/ 1/2 pint double pouring cream

1 punnet blueberries
Juice of half a lime
1 tablespoon caster sugar
1 tablespoon water

- Put wine, sherry, lime juice, water and sugar in a bowl. Stir and leave overnight.
- Simmer the blueberries, lime juice and sugar gently until cooked and some blueberries are left whole.
- Remove the whole blueberries and set aside. Liquidise the rest to a thick puree.
- Stir the cream slowly into the wine mixture.
- Whisk until soft peaks form.
- In a syllabub glass put a spoonful of cream followed by a little blueberry puree.
- Repeat leaving cream on the surface and place 3 or 4 whole blueberries in the centre. Serve with small dainty spoons.

The syllabub can be made in advance and keeps several days in the fridge.

Blueberry Buttermilk Pancakes with Maple Syrup

These are fat pancakes the size of a saucer which are suitable for a meal or as a breakfast-time treat.

175g/6oz self-raising flour
1 carton buttermilk
1 egg
Maple syrup
Butter
1 punnet blueberries

- Put the flour in a mixing bowl, together with the egg and gradually add the buttermilk.
- Add a little maple syrup, then fold in the blueberries. The mixture should be thicker than normal pancakes, but still be able to be dropped from a spoon.
- Melt a knob of butter in a frying pan and when nut brown carefully ladle in a spoonful or two of the mixture.
- Fry for 4 minutes on each side, turning over carefully. Serve on warm plates with plenty of maple syrup and a knob of butter.

Blueberry and Poppy Seed Lemon Drizzle Cake

This is a delicious cake with great flavour. The blueberries make it rather moist.
It is best eaten the day after cooking.

1 scant punnet of blueberries
2 lemons or limes
250g/9oz self-raising flour
250g/9oz golden caster sugar
1 large egg
1 teaspoon baking powder
100ml/3 $1/2$ fl oz single cream
55g/2oz soft butter
2 tablespoons Greek yoghurt
2 $1/2$ tablespoons poppy seeds

- Pre-heat oven to 350F/180C/Gas Mark 4.
- Grease and line with baking parchment 2 x 1lb loaf tins or 1 x 2lb tin.
- Grate zest from one lemon or lime.
- Put flour, butter, lemon zest, 200g/7oz sugar, baking powder, egg, cream and poppy seeds in a bowl. Process for several minutes with a hand-held electric mixer or food processor.
- Spoon half the mixture into cake tins, sprinkling with blueberries. Cover with rest of mixture and level the top with a knife.
- Bake for 1 hour and insert a skewer to see if it comes out clean. If the cake is getting too brown, cover with tin foil.
- Squeeze the lemon or lime juice in to a saucepan adding the remaining sugar 55g/2oz. Boil for 5 minutes.
- Remove tins from oven and prick all over with a cocktail stick.
- Spoon the syrup over the cake and leave to cool in tins. Freezes well.

Blueberry Almond Honey Cake

175g/6oz unsalted butter (soft)
175g/6oz caster sugar
4 eggs
250g/9oz ground almonds
100g/3 1/2 oz flaked almonds
A few drops almond essence (pure)
2 teaspoons baking powder
1 punnet blueberries
Heather honey
Crème fraiche

- Butter a 20cm x 5cm loose-bottomed cake tin and place a circle of baking parchment on the bottom of the tin. Pre-heat the oven to 190C/375F/Gas mark 5.
- Beat the butter and sugar together with an electric whisk until light and fluffy. Add the egg yolks and almond extract then fold in the ground almonds and baking powder.
- Whisk the egg whites until stiff and fold into the mixture with a metal spoon three times.
- Spoon half the mixture into the cake tin.
- Carefully arrange the blueberries on top and spoon the remaining mixture over the surface.
- Level with a knife and bake for 40-45 minutes until firm and golden.
- Leave in the tin for 10 minutes and run a knife around the edge turning out carefully.
- Dry fry the almonds in a frying pan until golden.
- Heat 2 tablespoons heather honey in a small saucepan. Spread honey over the top and sides of the cake. Cover both surfaces with the almonds leaving no honey showing - it is probably easier to tackle the sides first.
Serve with crème fraiche or mascarpone - excellent as a dessert.

COURGETTES

Courgette, Coconut and Dill Soup

900g/2lbs courgettes
1 onion
1 clove of garlic
1 potato (peeled)
1.2 litres/2 pints vegetable or chicken stock
3 tablespoons chopped dill
2 tablespoons olive oil
1 tin coconut milk or double Cream to swirl
Sea salt and freshly milled black pepper

- Heat oil in a saucepan, add chopped onion and crushed garlic, frying until soft but not coloured.
- Add sliced courgettes and chopped potato and stock.
- Simmer until soft.
- Process in a blender to a puree, adding coconut milk, dill and seasoning. Garnish with sprigs of dill. This is good either hot or cold.

Courgette and Green Pepper Brochettes

- Make a marinade with 2 crushed garlic cloves, salt, pepper, grated ginger, 2 teaspoons runny honey, chopped herbs such as rosemary or thyme, 2 tablespoons red wine vinegar.
- Marinade neatly chopped de-seeded peppers and thickly sliced courgettes. Thread onto skewers brushing well with marinade.
- Grill or barbeque until browned.
- Serve with barbecued meat or a plate of couscous.

Courgette Ribbons

A pretty way to serve courgettes is as follows:
- Peel thin strips (ribbons) from the courgette using a potato peeler.
- Cook gently in a frying pan with butter, adding seasoning and finely chopped parsley or snipped chives. This can be served with fish, meat or pasta.

Courgette and Olive Frittata (Serves 3)

4-5 eggs
3 spring onions
10 green stoned olives (stuffed with anchovies if possible)
75g/3oz grated parmesan
3 courgettes
Olive oil
A few rosemary leaves (finely chopped)
Seasoning

- Slice the courgettes fairly thinly and slice the spring onions including the green ends.
- Beat the eggs with the seasoning, add the parmesan and stir well.
- Slice the olives into 3.
- Put a generous amount of olive oil in a frying pan and when hot, arrange the courgette slices. Turn each one over when lightly browned and cook the other side then remove from pan and add the spring onions.
- When softened, return the courgettes to the pan and add the eggs, cooking until there is a firm crust on the bottom.
- Make holes in the mixture similar to cooking an omelette.
- Add the sliced olives and rosemary.
- One can either put the pan under a hot grill for a few minutes or serve straight away.
- Cut into portions.
  This is very good for a picnic as well as a light lunch or supper dish.

Little Courgette Fritters

300g/10 1/2 oz courgettes
100g/3 1/2 oz self raising flour
2 eggs (lightly beaten)
2 fl oz/50ml milk
Seasoning
Fresh thyme leaves or chopped rosemary leaves

- Grate the courgettes into a bowl, leave for 15 minutes then squeeze dry, extracting as much liquid as possible.
- Make a batter with flour, eggs and milk.
- Add the herb leaves and finally stir in the grated courgettes.
- Fry dessertspoons of the batter mixture in hot olive oil, turning over to the other side when bubbles appear.
- Keep warm in the oven until all are cooked.
- Serve hot as a 'nibble' for drinks, garnished with a courgette flower or rosemary sprig.

Erika's Special Caponata (Serves 8)

3 sticks green celery
2 shallots
4 large vine tomatoes
2 long sweet red peppers
1 large aubergine
2/3 courgettes
1 tablespoon red wine vinegar
2 tablespoons olive oil
2 tablespoons yellow sultanas
2 tablespoons pine nuts
1 tablespoons capers
Salt, freshly milled black pepper

This is best diced very small and cooked in a wok.

- Cut the celery sticks into four strips and dice, de-seed the peppers and dice small. Cut shallots into tiny dice and aubergine into small chunks. Treat the courgettes as celery sticks.
- Heat the oil in the wok adding shallots and aubergine.
- Stir fry without browning. Add the peppers, followed by tomatoes and vinegar. Put the lid on wok and cook gently until tomatoes have gone soft.
- Add seasoning, sultanas, capers and pine nuts, and courgettes. The courgettes must keep firm and crunchy.
- Cook until any liquid has evaporated.
- Put in plastic lidded container and chill.

This is lovely with parma ham and ciabatta bread, and can be used as a topping for bruschetta.

Terrine of Courgette and Spinach with Tomato Coulis
(Serves 6)

This is a lovely starter, or alternatively a light lunch served with salad and baby potatoes.

750g/1¾ lb courgettes
12 large spinach leaves
3 egg yolks, 1 white
300ml/10fl oz/ ½ pint double cream
Salt and freshly milled black pepper
A scant dessertspoon grain mustard.

- Trim courgettes and grate into a large bowl using a coarse grater.
- Blanch the spinach leaves for a few minutes in boiling water and refresh in cold water.
- Beat the eggs lightly, adding the seasoning and mustard and fold in the cream.
- Grease a loaf tin and line with cling film, then spinach leaves (patted dry with kitchen paper) allowing leaves to hang over the side of the tin.
- Squeeze liquid from the courgettes and mix with egg mixture.
- Spoon into the tin, and fold over the spinach, adding more leaves to cover.
- Place the tin in a baking tin half filled with water and place in a pre-heated moderate oven for 40 minutes until firm to touch.
- Refrigerate overnight.
- Drain any liquid and remove clingfilm. Cut into slices. Serve with Tomato Coulis (page 38)

THIS FRESH TASTING TERRINE IS A PERFECT VEGETARIAN OPTION. IT REALLY SEEMS STRAIGHT FROM THE GARDEN.

Mushroom Stuffed Courgettes

This is delicious on its own as a vegetarian meal, or to accompany grills.

4-6 courgettes
175g/6oz mushrooms
1-2 shallots (finely chopped)
60g/2oz Gruyere or Emmental cheese (grated)
1 1/2 cups milk
1 dessert spoon corn flour
Salt and pepper
Olive oil

- Rub the courgettes with olive oil. Cut in half lengthways and carefully scoop out the seeds with a teaspoon.
- Fry the shallots in a spoonful of olive oil.
- Remove from pan and add finely chopped button mushrooms and cook gently.
- Put in a bowl with the shallots and mix.
- Place the courgettes in an ovenproof dish and carefully spoon the mushrooms into the shells.
- Make a sauce with milk and a knob of butter and seasoning. When milk is hot add a little corn flour mixed with water and stir until fairly thick, adding the cheese.
- Carefully spoon over the mushrooms and bake in a moderate oven for 15-20 minutes.

A CRUMB TOPPING (optional)

Fry some fresh brown breadcrumbs in oil or butter until crisp and golden. Spoon over the courgettes just before serving so that the crumbs retain their crispness.

Tomato Coulis

Cook together tomatoes, orange juice and grated rind, salt and pepper until soft, adding more juice if required. Liquidise and serve in a small jug.

GARDENING TIPS FOR COURGETTES

Courgettes require lots of sun and a sheltered position. Make a recess around the plant with a trowel and fill with water.
Harvest the courgettes and flowers (which can be stuffed) when 4 inches long, cutting with a sharp knife. This will encourage new growth.
They can be grown in a large pot or a halved wooden beer barrel.

LAVENDER

'WHO WILL BUY MY SWEET LAVENDER'
Old London Street Cry

To pick Lavender

For culinary purposes only use
ENGLISH LAVENDER – the French Lavender
is not suitable. Pick only on sunny days, preferably
mid morning and just before the flowers open.

Lavender Salt

Grind absolutely dry lavender buds with sea salt
and store in a jar with a non-metallic lid. A very
subtle flavour for vegetables – and for where
salt has to be sprinkled, e.g. hard boiled
quails eggs.

DO NOT USE!

French Lavender

English Lavender

Lavender Sugar

- Choose flowers in full bloom and pick off each individual flower for a good colour.
- Grind (or use a pestle and mortar) 2 cups of petals and 2 cups preserving or granulated sugar.
- Spread on a baking tray lined in aluminium foil and dry for several hours in a very low heated oven.
- Break up the sugar and when cold store in a jar in a dark dry place.
  This is good in baking or sprinkled on desserts. Lasts a year.

Lavender Cream

10fl ozs/ 1/2 pint double or whipping cream
1 dessertspoon icing sugar
1 dessertspoon lavender buds

- Whip cream until soft, add icing sugar to taste.
- Fold in ground lavender buds - they can be pounded in a pestle and mortar, or ground in a food mill.
  This is good served with pies, fruit, etc.

Roast Lamb with Lavender

A rolled shoulder of lamb
Honey (preferably lavender honey)
2 cloves of garlic
Salt, freshly milled black pepper
8 lavender sprigs

- Smear lamb with honey, adding salt and pepper.
- Add chopped cloves of garlic and lavender flowers taken off the lavender sprigs. They should stick to the honey.
- Roast in a moderately hot oven, turning heat down towards the end for 1hr, 20 mins.
- Allow to rest.
- Skim any fat from the gravy.
- Serve with green beans and flageolets.
  See GREEN BEANS

Erika's Lavender Honeycomb

20fl oz/1 pint whole milk
1 tablespoon double cream
1 1/2 tablespoons caster sugar
2 eggs + 1 yolk
6 heads lavender
1 sachet powdered gelatine,
+ 1 teaspoon from another sachet
Peel from half a lemon

- Heat the milk, cream, sugar, lemon peel (use a potato peeler) and lavender until hot but not boiling.
- Leave to cool and infuse.
- Re-heat again and leave until lukewarm - adjust sugar.
  - Separate the eggs, whisk the yolks and add the milk straining through a sieve.
  - Press lemon and lavender against the sieve to extract as much flavouring as possible.
- Pour into a double boiler with hot water, and stir until the mixture thickens slightly - cool
- Melt gelatine in 1 1/2 tablespoons water until dissolved then add to cooled lavender mixture.
- Beat egg whites until stiff, and with a metal spoon carefully stir into custard.
  - Pour into wetted jelly moulds or small pudding basins then chill overnight in the fridge.
  - Turn out and sprinkle with a few lavender flowers.

THIS IS A FEATHER-LIGHT DESSERT WITH A VERY SUBTLE FLAVOUR. A JELLY-LIKE LAYER SEPARATES FROM THE REST WHICH IS NORMAL.

Erika's Crunchy Little Lavender and Pine nut Cakes

175g/6oz self-raising flour
1 teaspoon baking powder
25g/1oz yellow sultanas
125g/4 1/2 oz butter (soft)
50g/2oz pine nuts
125g/4 1/2 oz demerara sugar
1 egg
Vanilla essence
1 1/2 tablespoons lavender flower buds (freshly picked)

- Rub butter, flour and baking powder together.
- Add sugar, lavender, sultanas and pine nuts
- Beat egg and drops of vanilla and mix everything together with a fork.
- Put small heaps on a baking tray lined with baking parchment - use a teaspoon for this.
- Carefully sprinkle a little extra Demerara sugar on each mound.
- Bake in a pre-heated oven at 180C/350F/Gas 4 for 10 minutes.
- Carefully lift with a spatula onto a wire rack.

They look pretty served piled high on a small basket or plate with lots of lavender sprigs.

Some extra Lavender ideas

Pancakes

Add 1½ tablespoons lavender buds to pancake batter. Spread pancakes with lavender honey before rolling up. Spike with a stalk and head of lavender.

Scones

Add lavender flowers to scone mixture and serve with clotted cream and jam.

Shortbread

Add flower buds to mixture. Cut into shapes and sprinkle with lavender sugar.

Vinegar

Add 6 flower heads to bottle of white wine vinegar and keep in sun. After 3 weeks remove heads and replace with new ones.

Creme Brulee

Add 8 heads to cream when cooking and strain.

THE WONDERFUL SMELL OF A BED OF ENGLISH LAVENDER ENTRANCES THE SENSES. IT IS MARVELLOUS TO COMBINE IT WITH FOOD - SO SPECIAL, SO POETIC, AND SO MEMORABLE.

Erika's Lavender and Roasted Fig Ice-cream

4 figs
2 tablespoons lavender honey
1½ tablespoons fresh lavender buds
8 egg yolks
20fl oz/1pint double cream

- Roast halved figs smeared with honey in the oven or under a grill until juices run and figs are slightly caramelized.
- When cold chop finely, reserving all the juices.
- Heat cream with an extra spoonful of lavender honey and the lavender.
- Pour onto beaten egg yolks (after straining), transfer to a double boiler and cook over hot water until the mixture thickens.
- Add the chopped figs and juice and extra lavender buds.
- Freeze in freezer, or ice-cream maker. If possible, when serving spike a lavender head into the ice-cream.

GARDENING TIPS FOR LAVENDER

Lavender needs a sunny position and well drained soil. Not too much water as it originated in the Mediterranean. It prefers chalky soil but will grow in any garden soil.
After flowering, cut off faded flowers leaving 2/3 leaves below.

MINT

Erika's special Tomato, Mint and Orange Soup

1 kg /2 1/4 lbs tomatoes (vine preferably)
2 potatoes, peeled and sliced
1 onion, chopped
150ml /5fl oz fresh orange juice
2 oranges, grated rind
Small bunch fresh mint, chopped
Salt, freshly milled black pepper
A little water

- Skin tomatoes and remove pips.
- Chop and place in a large saucepan with the remaining ingredients.
- Cook gently until soft.
- Liquidise and taste, adding more juice or mint as required.
- Put in a container in the fridge.
- Serve cold with ice cubes, a swirl of double cream and a scattering of chopped mint leaves.
    If hot, add a knob of butter to each bowl so that it can be stirred in at the last minute.

Slow Roast Leg or Shoulder of Lamb with Dates and Couscous

1 leg or shoulder of lamb
Salt and freshly ground black pepper
2 cloves of garlic

COUSCOUS
225g/ 8oz couscous
850ml/1½ pints boiling water
100g /3½ oz blanched almonds, chopped and toasted
100g/3½ oz raisins or sultanas
175g/6oz dates, stoned and chopped
1½ tablespoons orange flower water
1 tablespoon ground cinnamon
110g/4oz melted butter
Stoned dates, blanched almonds, pomegranate seeds and chopped mint to decorate.

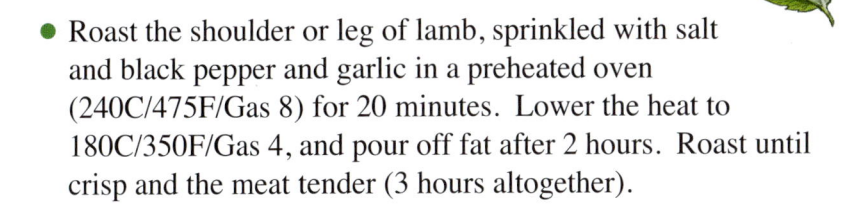

- Roast the shoulder or leg of lamb, sprinkled with salt and black pepper and garlic in a preheated oven (240C/475F/Gas 8) for 20 minutes. Lower the heat to 180C/350F/Gas 4, and pour off fat after 2 hours. Roast until crisp and the meat tender (3 hours altogether).

- Place the couscous in a bowl with the boiling water, salt, pepper, almonds, raisins or sultanas, dates, orange flower water and cinnamon. Stir well, and before serving add the melted butter.

- Decorate with extra dates filled with almonds. Sprinkle the dish with extra cinnamon, pomegranate seeds and chopped mint.

Iced Mint and Cucumber Soup

- In a bowl spoon a carton (454g) of Greek yoghurt.
- Add 2 1/2 tablespoons currants, 2 tablespoons chopped mint, a peeled, de-seeded and coarsely grated cucumber, half a grated onion, salt and freshly ground black pepper.
- Add iced water and ice cubes to dilute as required.

THIS IS A FANTASTIC REFRESHING SOUP FOR THE HOTTEST DAY OF THE YEAR. IT PRESSES ALL THE BUTTONS!

Baby Vegetables with Mint

Choose a selection of baby vegetables from the following: Tiny new potatoes, baby carrots, courgettes, sweetcorn, green beans, broad beans, turnips.

- Steam individually, and refresh in cold water.
- Before serving, put 2-3 tablespoons water and 50g/1 3/4 oz butter, salt, freshly milled black pepper in a shallow pan and heat.
- Warm the vegetables in the solution and add 2-3 tablespoons chopped fresh mint.
Note: the vegetables can be steamed well in advance.

Pineapple with Mint (serves 6)

- Prepare a pineapple by topping and tailing and cutting away all the outside skin.
- Cut into very thin slices and chill.
- Just before serving, sprinkle with a mint and sugar mixture. Mint and Sugar Mixture - pick the leaves off the stalks from a bunch of fresh mint, then put in a food processor with some caster sugar and whizz to a lovely green mixture.

Extra Special Couscous

1 cup couscous
1 tablespoon butter
1/2 red onion (finely diced)
3 plum tomatoes (seeded and diced)
1/2 cup mint (finely chopped)
1/2 cup flat leaf parsley (finely chopped)
1/2 cup coriander leaves (finely chopped)
2 tablespoons preserved lemon (diced)
1 tablespoon lemon juice
3 tablespoons olive oil
1 400g tin/14oz rinsed chick peas
Pomegranate seeds
Cinnamon
Pinenuts

- Put couscous in a large bowl with the butter.
- Cover with 1 cup boiling water and leave for 30 minutes.
- Separate grains with a fork.
- Mix everything together with sea salt and freshly milled black pepper.
- Spoon onto a serving platter, drizzle with melted butter and lightly sprinkle with powdered cinnamon.
- Scatter pomegranate seeds as a colourful decoration and, if liked, toasted pinenuts.

Grandmother's 'Herby' Yorkshire Pudding

THIS IS DIFFERENT TO THE NORMAL VERSION. IT IS EXCELLENT SERVED COLD CUT INTO LARGE SQUARES AND TOPPED WITH SLICES OF COLD BEEF, LAMB OR CHICKEN. PERFECT FOR PICNICS - BUT ALSO GOOD WITH HOT ROAST BEEF.

1 slice wholemeal bread
1 onion (finely sliced and chopped)
2 eggs
115g/4oz self-raising flour
200ml/7floz milk
Seasoning
Chopped herbs such as flat leaf parsley, mint, thyme
Dripping

- Soak bread in milk and when soft squeeze dry and crumble.
- Fry onions until just soft and reserve.
- Put the flour in a bowl with the seasoning.
- Beat the eggs slightly and add to the flour followed by the milk.
- Stir in the onions, herbs and bread and allow to stand for 30 minutes.
- Pre-heat oven to 220 °C/425° F/Gas 7 and place a rectangular roasting tin with some dripping or corn oil in - when hot add the 'herby' batter.
- Bake for 15-20 minutes until brown and well risen.
- Cut into neat squares and serve with appropriate sauces - Horseradish with beef, mint with lamb or for chicken, a sauce made with mayonnaise, curry powder and puréed apricots.

Erika's Pepper, Chilli and Mint Chutney

1½kg/3lbs Bramley cooking apples, peeled and chopped
4 large green peppers, de-seeded and chopped
250g/9oz yellow sultanas
2 onions, finely chopped
1kg/2lbs golden granulated sugar
1 red chilli pepper, de-seeded and finely chopped
425ml/ ¾ pint cider vinegar
Salt
2 handfuls of chopped fresh mint (no stalks)

Simmer all together until thick, adding mint towards the end.

Home-made Mint Tea

This is delicious and very good for the digestion. Put a handful of mint leaves into a teapot and also 1½ tablespoons caster sugar.
Add boiling water and allow to stand.

MINTY GARDENING TIPS

Mint tends to spread everywhere so it is a good idea to grow in a large pot and keep by the back door or in a window-box.

Plant mint plants in a large pot with broken bits of terracotta flower pots, a few bits of barbeque charcoal and soil.

It is a good idea to cut the mint stalks to 2 inches above soil level when it gets leggy. This will make the mint shoot again with new growth.

A good time to pick mint (Mentha spicata/Spearmint) for freezing, preserving or drying is just before flowering when the aroma is at its strongest.

THE WONDERFUL AROMA OF FRESH MINT REMINDS ME OF A HOT SUMMER'S DAY, SITTING IN A SHADY SPOT WITH A TALL GLASS OF PIMMS BRIMMING WITH ICE AND MINT SPRIGS IMPARTING THEIR DELICIOUS FLAVOUR.

PEAS

There was an old person of Dean
Who dined on one pea and a bean,
For he said, 'More than that
Would make me too fat',
That cautious old person of Dean.

Edward Lear 1812-1888

Iced Green Pea and Lettuce Soup (Serves 4-6)

Fresh or frozen peas
Good chicken stock
1 potato, peeled and chopped
1 onion, peeled and chopped
Half an Iceberg lettuce
Seasoning
Double cream to drizzle

- Cook all the ingredients until soft.
- Liquidise, cool and refrigerate.
- Pour into bowls with a garnish of a little shredded lettuce and a drizzle of cream. This can also be served hot, minus the shredded lettuce.

Mushy Pea Soup with Ham (Serves 4-5)

450g/1lb marrowfat peas (soaked in cold water overnight)
A small ham bone (cooked)
3 celery sticks, finely chopped
1 carrot and 1 onion
Water to cover
Seasoning
Milk or cream

- Cut any fatty pieces off the bone and put in a large saucepan with plenty of water together with drained peas. Cook for 45 minutes.
- Remove bone and partially liquidise the peas with the stock.
- Add celery, chopped carrot and onion and seasoning and cook until vegetables are soft.
- Add diced ham pieces, a little milk or cream and heat through.

Curried Pea Puree

450g/1lb fresh or frozen peas
5fl oz/ 1/4 pint double cream
Salt
1 1/2 dessertspoons curry powder

- Cover peas with boiling water and cook for 5 minutes until tender.
- Drain and liquidise, adding salt and curry powder to taste. This is good served with white fish or chicken.
- Dilute with more cream to turn purée into a Curried Pea Sauce.

Erika's Pea Mousse with Prawns (Serves 6)

This makes a pretty starter.

800g/1 ¾ lb frozen garden peas
Half a chicken stock cube
3 tablespoons thick double cream
1¼ sachets powdered gelatine
Large prawns to garnish
Pea shoots to garnish
Crispy bacon to garnish
2 egg whites

- Cook peas for 6 minutes with enough boiling water to cover, adding stock cube. Drain liquid into a jug and liquidise the peas then pass through a sieve or chinois.
- Mix gelatine with half a mug of pea liquid and heat in a saucepan of hot water until melted.
- Stir into lukewarm pea purée, together with cream.
- Beat egg whites until stiff and gently fold, using a metal spoon, into the pea mixture adding seasoning to taste.
- Spoon into little individual ramekins which have been rinsed in cold water. Refrigerate and chill until set.
- Turn out onto individual plates.
- Arrange prawns mixed with chilli and coriander on top. Garnish with broken 'crispy' bacon, and a sprig of pea shoot on one side.
(Not too much greenery!).

Lemon, Chilli and Pea Spaghetti (Serves 4)

350g/12oz spaghetti
250g/9oz frozen young peas
1 green or red chilli, finely chopped
Grated rind 2 lemons, juice of 1 lemon
75g/3 oz grated parmesan (fresh if possible)
2 1/2 tablespoons olive oil
Sea salt and freshly milled black pepper

- Grate lemon rind into a large bowl, add the juice, olive oil, parmesan and seasoning. Mix together.
- Lightly fry the chopped de-seeded chilli and add to the bowl.
- Cook spaghetti in boiling water according to packet instructions - at the same time cook the peas in boiling water for 5 minutes and drain, blotting dry with kitchen paper.
- Drain the pasta and add to the lemon mixture together with peas.
- Stir quickly and serve.

Mangetout Peas with Prawns (Serves 4)

350g/12oz mangetout peas, ends removed
300g/10 1/2 oz peeled prawns
3 cloves of garlic (chopped)
2 shallots, peeled and chopped
1 inch fresh ginger, peeled and grated
1 green chilli, de-seeded and finely chopped
Juice 1 lime
Sea salt
1 dessertspoon palm sugar, or soft brown
1 1/2 tins coconut milk

- Lightly fry, without browning, shallots, garlic, ginger and chilli.
- Add mangetouts which can be cut in half on the slant.
- Add coconut milk and lime juice and simmer gently until mangetouts are cooked.
- Stir in prawns and a little salt and warm through, adding more coconut milk if necessary.
- Serve together with Jasmine rice.
- Grease a small jelly mould or teacup with butter and fill with rice, pressing down.
- Turn out onto plate and surround with prawns and mangetouts.

For a gastronomic touch, dry fry some desiccated coconut, 1 tablespoon caster sugar and cayenne pepper and sprinkle around the outside of the plate.

French Peas with Veal or Duck (Serves 4)

These peas are served with most dishes in France and are delicious.

450g/1lb small petit pois peas (larger ones can be used)
6-8 trimmed spring onions
1 dessertspoon caster sugar
Salt, freshly ground black pepper
6 little Gem lettuces (or 3 halved)
A little butter

- Layer the peas, onions, lettuce and butter and cover with a little water.
- Gently simmer for 30-40 minutes until the majority of the liquid has evaporated.
- Give 1 lettuce and 1 spring onion per person. Serve with roast duck or grilled duck breast – or roast veal or pan fried veal chop.

Pea Dip

This is good for aperitifs or with a dish of crudities.

200g/7oz podded peas
150ml/5 fl oz/ 1/2 pint mayonnaise
200g/7oz full fat cream cheese
Grated rind of 1 lemon
Juice of 1/2 lemon
Freshly milled black pepper
Salt to taste

Cook the peas, liquidise and sieve.
Mix with the cream cheese, seasoning, lemon rind and juice.
Fold in the mayonnaise.
Note: If a minty dip is preferred, stir in 2 teaspoons of mint sauce.

Grandmother's Pea Sandwiches

Cook and mash some fresh garden peas. When cold add good quality softened butter and seasoning. Spread on very fresh country white bread. Cut off crusts or pile high 'canape' style on small pieces, or on bruschetta.

PEAS ARE SUCH A POPULAR VEGETABLE ONE CAN NEVER TIRE OR HAVE ENOUGH OF THEM. ONE OF CHILDHOOD'S MYSTERIES IS FIRST MASTERING THE SKILL OF BALANCING PEAS ON A FORK! REMEMBER?

PEAS HAVE BEEN AROUND SINCE THE ANCIENT EGYPTIANS!

GARDENING TIPS FOR PEAS

Peas are quite easy to grow trained up wigwams in pots. Pea seedlings and mangetout seedlings can be obtained in most garden centres.

Peas germinate more quickly if soaked in water for 2 hours before planting in summer. Apply seaweed spray.

Pea tops or pea shoots (obtainable at some supermarkets) can be snipped when peas are 14 days old. They are excellent as a garnish, in a salad or stir fry. The leaves taste like peas!

RASPBERRIES

Raspberry Jelly with Creamy Custard (Serves 4)

250g /9oz raspberries
3 tablespoons caster sugar
1 sachet gelatine
3 egg yolks
Caster sugar
A vanilla pod or 3 teaspoons vanilla bean paste
170ml/ 6fl oz double cream
300ml/10fl oz/ 1/2 pint single cream
1 tablespoon milk
1 spoonful cornflour

- Press the raspberries through a sieve to remove pips.
- Add the sugar and leave for half an hour to dissolve.
- Melt the gelatine with 1 tablespoon water in a cup over simmering water. Stir into the raspberry puree.
- Pour into a rectangular tinfoil container which has been rinsed in cold water. Chill overnight in the fridge.
- Turn out onto a board and cut into half inch strips, then into squares or diamonds or, if you own them, use heart shaped cutters. Keep aside for the custard - they must be small and pretty.
- Scoop the seeds from a split vanilla pod, put them together with the cream and sugar and simmer gently.
- Remove seeds, add the beaten egg yolks and cook very gently.
- Thicken with a spoonful of cornflour mixed with milk. Chill overnight.
- To serve, pour the custard into glass bowls or dishes. Place the raspberry squares or diamonds or hearts prettily over the custard.

RASPBERRY JELLY IS A LOVELY DESSERT FOR EVERYONE INCLUDING CHILDREN AND THE ELDERLY. THE RASPBERRY SHAPES ARE A SURPRISE FLOATING ON THE CREAMY CUSTARD.

Raspberry Alaska (Serves 6-8)

700g/1½ lbs raspberries
425 ml/15 fl oz/ ¾ pint double cream
100g /3 ½ oz caster sugar
4 egg whites
175g /6oz caster sugar
A sponge cake from recipes in this book

- Press the raspberries through a sieve.
- Add the sugar and the softly whipped double cream and pour into a lidded plastic pudding basin lined in clingfilm and put in the freezer. Alternatively use an ice-cream machine before putting in the container.
- Remove from freezer, peel off the clingfilm and put on cake. Place cake and ice-cream on a wooden board.
- Whip the egg whites until fairly stiff, gradually adding sugar.
- Quickly swirl over ice-cream and place in a pre-heated oven 220C/425F/Gas 7 for 5 minutes until lightly browned.
- Transfer to a pretty plate.
- Have a bowl of sugared raspberries and redcurrants to serve with the Alaska.

Raspberry Hazelnut Meringue

This is a delicious dessert or birthday gateau and originates from Austria. If possible use wild raspberries which have more flavour.

175g/6oz shelled, roasted and ground hazelnuts
300g /10oz caster sugar
250g /9oz raspberries
300ml/10fl oz/ 1/2 pint double cream
5 egg whites
1 teaspoon white wine vinegar
Icing sugar or glucose to dust

- Line two 20 – 30cm (8 – 9 inch) loose bottomed sandwich tins with parchment and heat oven to 180C/350F/Gas 4
- Whisk egg whites until stiff, adding sugar gradually and finally the vinegar.
- Fold hazelnuts gently into the mixture using a metal spoon.
- Spoon into the tins and bake 35-40 minutes.
- Leave until cold.
- Just before serving, peel parchment carefully off the meringue and place on a suitable plate, then whip the cream until soft peaks form and spread onto one half.
- Cover with raspberries, pressing into the cream.
- Place the other hazelnut meringue on top and sprinkle with glucose or icing sugar.

Tarte Cardinale (serves 6)

- Line a flan dish with rich shortcrust pastry adding 2 1/2 teaspoons ground cinnamon and bake blind. When cold fill the flan case with 900g/2lbs strawberries pointed ends facing upwards, and tightly packed.
- Make a puree from 450g/1lb sieved raspberries mixed with 225g/8oz sieved icing sugar.
- Spoon over the strawberries.
- These quantities are for 11 inch flans – adjust ingredients when using smaller or larger dishes.

Raspberry Vinegar

1 1/2 kg/3lb raspberries
850ml/1 1/2 pints white wine vinegar

- Put 450g/1lb raspberries in a wide necked jar with a non-metallic cover.
- Leave in a sunny place for 3 – 4 days shaking occasionally.
- Strain the liquid into another jar and add a second 450g/1lb raspberries, repeating the process.
- Strain the liquid again and add the final 450g /1lb raspberries.
- Strain and bottle.
  The liquid should be a beautiful cardinal red colour. It is wonderful for delicate salads and for de-glazing pans of steak, gammon, veal, calves liver and duck breasts.

Fresh Summery Raspberry Mousse (Serves 4)

225g/8oz raspberries
2 tablespoons caster sugar
3 tablespoons softly whipped double cream
3 1/2 tablespoons greek yoghurt
2 egg whites
3 sheets gelatine, broken into pieces
2 tablespoons boiling water
Raspberries to decorate (optional)

- Liquidise the raspberries in a blender and press through a sieve (chinois).
- Put the puree in a medium sized bowl and add the sugar, stirring well.
- Stir in the yoghurt followed by the whipped cream.
- Put the broken gelatine in a jug or bowl and cover with the boiling water.
- Allow to melt, stirring.
- Whisk the egg whites with a pinch of salt until they form stiff peaks.
- Stir the melted gelatine into the raspberry mixture, followed by the egg whites, folding gently.
- Spoon into tall, slim, long-stemmed glasses or small syllabub glasses.

THIS IS A LOVELY FRESH-TASTING DESSERT, A VERY PRETTY COLOUR AND VERY SUMMERY.
FOR AN ALTERNATIVE SERVING SUGGESTION, SPOON THE MOUSSE INTO SMALL DEMI-TASSE COFFEE CUPS AND DRIZZLE JUST A LITTLE RASPBERRY LIQUEUR (CRÈME DE FRAMBOISE) ON TOP. ADD A FEW RASPBERRIES TO THE SAUCER, A TEASPOON AND A TINY BISCUIT.

Lacy Raspberry Ice-cream Pancakes (Serves 4)

50g/2oz plain flour
A pinch of salt and a pinch of sugar
15g/ 1/2 oz melted butter
150ml/5 fl oz/ 1/4 pint milk
225g/8oz fresh raspberries
3 tablespoons Crème de Framboise
Sunflower oil
Vanilla ice-cream or marscapone
Icing sugar to garnish and, if possible, a raspberry leaf

- Put flour in a bowl and make a well in the centre - add the egg and milk, beating well.
- Stir in the melted butter, salt and sugar, beating to a cream like batter.
- Tip the raspberries into a small bowl and mix with the raspberry liquer.
- Heat oil in a small, non-stick frying or omelette pan, wiping away any excess with kitchen paper.
- Using a tablespoon, quickly drizzle batter into pan in a circle.
- Make lines with another tablespoonful and thick squiggles with another - this is not as difficult as it sounds!
- Turn over, using a fish slice, and place on a plate.
- Spoon some raspberries and liqueur into centre of the pancake.
- Add a scoop of vanilla ice-cream or marscapone and fold carefully in half.
- Sprinkle with sieved icing sugar and garnish with a raspberry leaf if you have one.

THIS DESSERT IS VERY PRETTY AND DAINTY AND EASY TO MAKE AS EVERYTHING IS PREPARED IN ADVANCE. OTHER FRUITS CAN BE SUBSTITUTED FOR RASPBERRIES, SUCH AS STRAWBERRIES OR NECTARINE SLICES.

For a Summer Drink

Measure 600ml/1pint raspberry vinegar and add 450g/1lb caster sugar. Put in a coated saucepan and heat to below boiling point for 10 minutes. When cold pour into small bottles and refrigerate. Use with ice cubes and soda water or lemonade.

Raspberry Scones

Mash together some ripe well-flavoured fresh raspberries with sugar or glucose.
Use instead of jam with clotted cream and warm scones.

Raspberry Champagne

Put some chilled and sweetened fresh raspberry puree in the base of a champagne flute together, if available, with a dash of raspberry liqueur.
Top up with champagne, or sparkling wine.

TIPS FOR COOKS : 1 lb raspberries = 1/2 pint puree

TRY HUNTING FOR WILD RASPBERRIES WHICH HAVE A WONDERFUL AROMA AND ARE MY FAVOURITE FRUIT!

GARDENING TIPS FOR RASPBERRIES

A few late fruiting raspberries are always a welcome fruit in the garden. I suggest 'Autumn Bliss' which is reasonably trouble-free. Also, they do not attract birds in the way that summer fruiting varieties do.

Choose a very big pot or half a beer barrel and fill the base with broken flower pots and a slightly acid soil. They do not grow in a heavy soil such as clay.

Plant in late autumn, making sure that the roots are 3 inches below the soil surface. Plant 15 inches apart.

Cut old canes down to 9 inches in late winter and thin out new growth gradually. The canes need support with a bamboo cane and require tying up. The plants flourish well in light shade and are happy with a mulch which keeps the moisture in.

ROSES

'WON'T YOU COME INTO THE GARDEN - I WOULD LIKE MY ROSES TO SEE YOU'

Richard Brinsley Sheridan 1751 - 1816

Use scented roses whenever possible in these recipes. Rosa Gallica, Alec's Red and Roseraie de l'Hay are preferable.

Rosa Gallica

Erika's Special Rose Summertime Sponge for Rozelle (serves 6-8)

(This makes a great birthday cake or dinner party gateau)

150g/5 1/2 oz plain flour, sieved with a pinch of salt and a pinch of baking powder
225g/8oz caster sugar
4 eggs
1 dessertspoon rose water
2 tablespoons unsprayed scented rose petals (white tips removed)
Whipped double cream
Icing sugar
Cochineal food colouring
Rose petal jam (see page 71)

- Prepare a 9 inch round cake tin by greasing and sprinkling with sugar and flour. Tip excess away and set oven to 175C/350F/G4
- Beat egg whites until stiff, beating in half the sugar.
- Beat egg yolks with rest of sugar until thick and pale, adding rosewater.
- Fold carefully into the egg whites with a metal spoon.
- Gradually add the flour folding gently.
  Add the rose petals and spoon into the cake tin.
- Bake for 30-35 minutes until firm, golden and well-risen.
- Turn out onto a wire rack and when cool slice into 2 or 3 layers.
- Spread one layer with rose petal jam, the other with whipped double cream and press the layers together.
- Spread with an icing made from icing sugar, rose water and a very little cochineal.
- Allow to drip down the sides and decorate with a beautiful pink rose and a few petals on the plate (sparklers and candles if a birthday or celebration).

Rose Petal Jam

This is not difficult to make and can be organised several days before making the cake.

3-4 heads of red/pink scented roses (unsprayed)
Juice of half a lemon
120g/4oz caster sugar

- Remove white tips from roses, and put in a saucepan with a little water and boil for 5 minutes.
- Add lemon juice and the colour will turn pink.
- Liquidise briefly, then add sugar and boil until setting point.

Rose Petal Sandwiches

These are a great surprise and very delicious.
Use strongly scented unsprayed pink or red garden roses, white tips of petals removed.

- Butter (using good, unsalted butter) very fresh and thinly sliced white bread. Place rose petals on top, sprinkling with caster sugar, and cover with another buttered slice and press together.
- Remove crusts and cut into tiny sandwiches. Keep in the fridge until required. Scatter a few rose petals on the plate.

Rosey Ice-Cream (serves 6-8)

8 egg yolks
425ml/15fl ozs/³/₄ pint double cream
50g/1³/₄ oz caster sugar
2 tablespoons rosewater
A few drops of cochineal
Pink Turkish Delight (chopped small)

- Whisk the egg yolks and sugar until thick.
- Transfer to a double-boiler or bowl over simmering hot water.
- Stir until thick, adding rosewater and allow to cool.
- Whip cream until nearly thick.
- Fold into egg mixture with the cochineal.
- Add the Turkish Delight and freeze.
  Serve in glass goblets and decorate with a small pink rosebud.

White Chocolate Rose Truffles

- Melt 200g/7oz white chocolate. very slowly in a bowl over gently simmering water.
- When melted add 1 tablespoon rosewater and a tiny drop of cochineal.
- Stir in 2 teaspoons runny honey and put in the fridge for 30 minutes.
- Scoop the mixture with a teaspoon and roll into small balls.
- Whizz in a food processor a pack of crystallized rose petals, and roll the chocolate balls in this.
  Attractive to serve with coffee.

ROSES ARE ROMANTIC, ROSES ARE SUMMERTIME, AND FOOD FLAVOURED WITH ROSES INSPIRES THE POETIC DREAMS IN US ALL..

Lamb Kebabs with Rose

Prepare lamb kebabs using lamb fillet.
Roll the kebabs in crushed coriander and
sprinkle with rose water and olive oil.
Grill as normal and before serving sprinkle with
freshly milled black pepper, salt and more rosewater.

Rose Vinegar

Fill a screw-top jar with red scented rose petals
removing the yellow tip which is bitter. Top up with
good quality white wine or cider vinegar.
Leave in the sun for 1 week - 10 days, shaking
occasionally.
Throw away the petals, squeezing the liquid well.
Refill the jar with fresh petals and leave as before.
Decant into suitable bottles.
This is a lovely rosy red colour.
It is rather an exclusive vinegar, so
I give it only to special guests!

GARDENING TIPS FOR ROSES

Use large containers such as half a wooden wine cask to give the rose plenty of root room. Use smaller pots for patio pots.
Put bricks under the tub or pot and broken pots in the base.
Fill with a soil-based compost (not peat) mixed with a little leaf mould and a sprinkle of bone meal.
Spray for greenfly, blackspot etc following the brand's instructions.
Deadhead the faded flower heads to promote new growth. Fertilise twice a year and give a mulch of manure or bark chippings.
Prune in February to keep the shape, removing suckers and dead wood.
Water well, but do not allow the soil to become soggy.

Curly Endive

Italian Red Dandelion

Lambs Lettuce

Red Mustard

SALAD LEAVES

O cool in the summer is salad
And warm in the winter is love –
Take endive – like love it is bitter,
Take beet – for like love it is red,
Crisp leaf of the lettuce shall glitter,
And cress from the riverlet's bed,
Anchovies, foam born, like the lady
Whose beauty has maddened this bard,
And olives, form the groves that are shady;
And eggs – boil 'em hard.

Mortimer Collins 1827-1876

THERE IS A GREAT VARIETY OF SALAD LEAVES ON THE MARKET– SOME ARE TASTIER THAN OTHERS – BUT THEY ARE ALL GOOD FOR US.

Some garnishes to add to green salads

- Deep fried crumbled crispy onion or grilled crumbed streaky bacon rashers make delicious garnishes.

- Try frying slivers of peeled fresh ginger cut into matchstick sized pieces and fried until crisp.

- Mimosa - hard boiled egg yolks sieved and sprinkled over the surface of a tossed green salad.

- French - use plain salad such as Webb's Wonder, Iceberg, Scarole, Chicory or Little Gem. Rub the salad bowl with garlic and also rub small pieces of French bread.

Make a classic French dressing with 3 tablespoons olive oil, 1 tablespoon red wine vinegar, a generous teaspoon of Dijon mustard. Toss the salad adding the garlic bread which will become damp with the dressing. Make sure everyone has a piece!

- Salad leaves can have interesting additions such as pomegranate seeds, toasted pinenuts, sliced radish, parmesan shavings, crispy fried cubed pancetta.

- Dressings can be made using double cream and lemon, vinaigrette made with cider or tarragon, or rose or raspberry or balsamic vinegar. Herbs such as snipped chives, tarragon or mint can be added to the salad.

- Rose petals, violets, primroses, clove pink petals, borage flowers and small viola flowers or pot marigold (calendula officinalis) petals make colourful and edible decorations.
  Do not use French Marigold.

- Dark leaves such as lambs lettuce, rocket, young spinach or watercress are a good garnish for pale foods such as eggs.

- Rocket is often used as a sophisticated and elegant garnish for pasta, risotto or pizza. Use a generous handful and pile on top of the dish.

PEA SHOOTS ARE A NEW SALAD INGREDIENT AND CAN BE FOUND IN MOST SUPERMARKETS. THEY ARE THE YOUNG LEAVES AND TENDRILS FROM MANGETOUT YOUNG PLANTS. THE TENDRILS LOOK VERY PRETTY AS A GARNISH AND TASTE OF PEAS.

Hazelnut Salad

Use hazelnut oil, raspberry vinegar, salt and freshly ground black pepper and chopped skinned roasted hazelnuts mixed with various salad leaves.

Walnut Salad with Pears

Use walnut oil, wine vinegar, salt and freshly ground black pepper and chopped roasted walnuts with chicory and rocket. Peeled sliced pears (first tossed in lemon juice) and pieces of blue cheese such as Roquefort make an excellent salad.

Orange Salad

This is good as an accompaniment to duck :

5 oranges
1 dessertspoon orange flower water
2 tablespoons olive oil
Salt and freshly ground black pepper
Sprinkle of ground cinnamon
Watercress and 1 fennel bulb

- Peel and slice the oranges into thin circles.

- Arrange watercress and finely sliced fennel on a plate.
- Lay the orange slices on top.
- Mix oil, orange flower water and seasoning together with any orange juice.
- Spoon over the oranges and sprinkle with cinnamon.

* A variation is black olives, thinly sliced red onion and sliced radishes.

Erika's Rose Salad

1 lettuce heart
2 tablespoons olive oil
1 tablespoon rose vinegar (see page 55)
Salt, freshly milled black pepper
Pink rose petals (white tips removed)

- Tear the lettuce heart.
- Mix the dressing and pour over salad.
- Mix with fingertips and scatter rose petals over the salad.
  This looks poetic and beautiful and is a lovely delicate salad.

Quails Egg Salad

5 quails eggs per person
Small salad leaves
2 punnets of cress
Carrots (grated into long strips)
Radishes (sliced or grated)
Smoked salmon or peeled shrimps
Mayonnaise

- Hard boil the quails eggs following the instructions on the box. Plunge into cold water and remove the shells - roll them about.
- Make 'nests' with the salad leaves, grated carrots and cress.
- Arrange the eggs in the nests.
- Cut the smoked salmon into 1/2 inch strips, roll up neatly and arrange around the eggs. Sprinkle with a little snipped dill.
- Gently sprinkle a very little celery salt on top of the eggs.
- Add a little grated radish for colour and spoon a light vinaigrette over the leaves just before serving.
- Serve a dainty bowl of mayonnaise on the side using fresh orange juice instead of lemon juices and a little snipped dill.
Note: Use only 3 eggs if serving as a starter.
This salad is also suitable for a light lunch or supper dish.
I often add 1 - 1 1/2 tablespoons of cold water to the vinaigrette for a lighter effect.

Roasted Vegetable Salad

Choose a colourful selection of vegetables and prepare for roasting.

Red and yellow peppers - halved, de-seeded and cut into four
Red onions - skinned and cut into four
Courgettes - cut in chunks on the slant
Aubergines - cut in slices
Tomatoes - cut in half
Small carrots - cut in chunks
Sweet potatoes- peeled and cut in chunks

- Rub all the vegetables in olive oil, sprinkle with sea salt and freshly ground black pepper.
- Sprinkle with lemon juice, sliced garlic (if liked) and thyme leaves or rosemary.
- Roast in a moderate oven until beginning to char at the edges.
- Arrange a colourful mixture of baby salad leaves and rocket on a serving platter or individual plates.
- Arrange the vegetables on top and sprinkle with toasted pinenuts and sprigs of basil or mint.
- Serve with garlic bread or sliced ciabatta bread spread with pesto sauce.

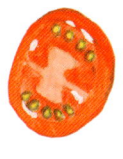

Fig or Nectarine Salad

This is suitable for a light lunch or supper.

- Cover a plate with rocket and other salad leaves.
- Tear slices of parma ham and arrange, also mozzarella cheese. Arrange slices of fig artistically.
- Sprinkle with sea salt and freshly milled black pepper.
- Drizzle with olive oil and balsamic vinegar (if possible fig balsamic), and sprinkle with dry fried pinenuts, and torn basil leaves.
- Serve with ciabatta bread or country bread.

GARDENING TIPS FOR SALAD LEAVES

LAMBS LETTUCE – CORN SALAD or MACHE
Easily grown in pots or window boxes. It self seeds if permitted and is ready to pick when four pairs of leaves appear. Will survive during winter.

SALAD BOWL A useful lettuce – one can pick the leaves when required and this does not damage the plant.

ROCKET Easy to grow and can be picked 4 – 12 weeks after planting. Leaves will sprout again several times after picking.

SPINACH and SWISS CHARD

Spinach and Smoked Haddock Soup
Serves 4

450g/1lb smoked haddock
675g/1½lbs spinach
Double or single cream
2 peeled, chopped potatoes
1 peeled, chopped onion
Seasoning and 1
chicken stock cube

- Gently cook haddock in a little milk.
- Cool and remove the skin and any bones.
- Cook onion and potato until soft in a little water and chicken stock cube.
- Add spinach and any haddock milk, and most of the haddock.
- Cook for 5 minutes until spinach has wilted.
- Liquidise and add the cream and some haddock flakes.

Spinach and Ricotta Tartlets

175g/4-6oz spinach, wilted, finely chopped and free of liquid
200g/7oz ricotta
2 tablespoons grated parmesan
Seasoning and grated nutmeg
2 lightly beaten eggs
4 tablespoons single or double cream
75g/3oz pine nuts

- Mix all the ingredients in a bowl until well blended.
- Divide the mixture between pre-cooked savoury pastry cases and sprinkle with pine nuts.
- Bake in pre-heated oven 200C/400F/Gas 6, for 10 minutes.
- Serve lukewarm.
  Pre-baked savoury tartlets in various sizes can be obtained in all good supermarkets. They are excellent and a good short-cut to making pastry.

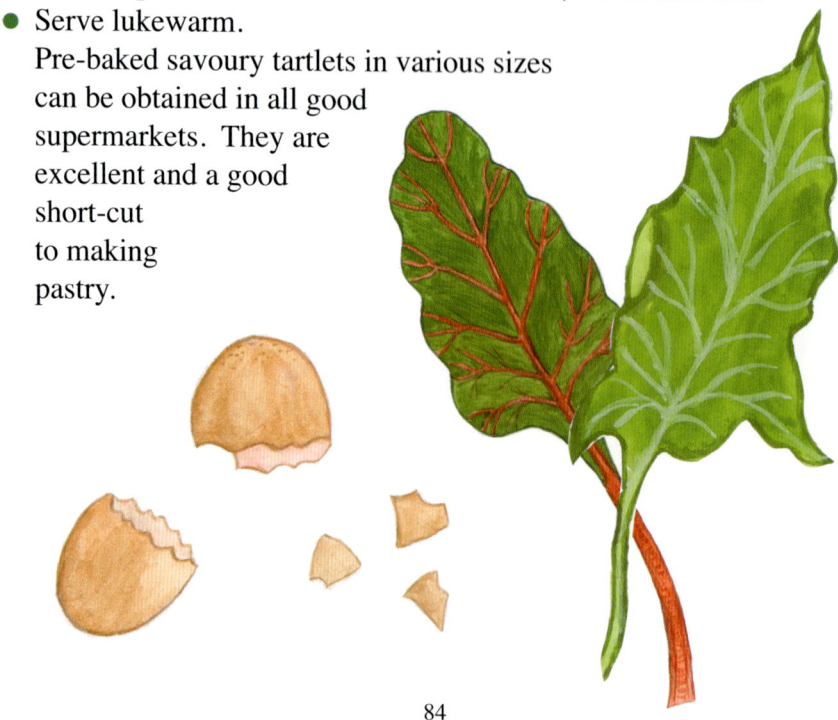

Spinach Ramekins
Serves 4

450g/1lb spinach
225g/8oz button mushrooms, quartered or sliced
25g/1oz butter
300ml/10fl oz / ½ pint double cream
4 eggs
Seasoning

- Grease ramekins with butter.
- Cook spinach, press out any water, chop, season and add a little butter.
- Fry mushrooms in butter, put spinach in each ramekin and top with mushrooms.
- Carefully crack an egg into each ramekin and mask with double cream.
- Bake in a moderate oven in a tin of water for 10 minutes, or in a frying pan on top of stove, or wok with water on top of stove, until eggs are set.

For a luxury touch, omit the mushrooms and add a small piece of duck liver pate.

I LOVE SPINACH AND EAT IT AS OFTEN AS POSSIBLE AS IT IS NUTRITIOUS, DELICIOUS, HAS IRON AND LOADS OF VITAMINS – THINK OF 'POPEYE'! IT WAS REPUTED TO GIVE HIM MUSCLES!
THE BEST FLAVOUR IS OF COURSE FROM YOUR OWN GARDEN.

Spinach, Cottage Cheese and Pineapple

This was a dish I tasted in New Zealand when a guest brought it to a barbecue.

1kg/2 1/4 lbs young spinach
1-2 tubs cottage cheese
2 tins of crushed pineapple (drained)
Or 3/4 of a peeled, cored and finely diced fresh pineapple
Seasoning and a spoonful olive oil

Mix all together and serve in a rustic looking dish.

Some little spinach ideas

- Puréed and mixed with cooked rice for a green rice
- Puréed and mixed in pancake batter
- Cooked, drained, mixed with fried mushrooms, cream and cheese on toasted ciabatta bread – or as a pancake stuffing.
- Made into a roulade
- A Moroccan stew with tomatoes, onions, raisins, chickpeas, paprika, ground cumin and ground cinnamon, salt and pepper.

Salad of Spinach and Feta Cheese
Serves 2-3

1kg/ 2 1/4 lbs spinach, cooked and drained
200g/7oz feta cheese (crumbled)
175g/6oz flaked almonds (dry fried)
225g/8oz cherry tomatoes, halved
Salt, freshly milled black pepper
Olive oil and lemon quarters to serve

- Place spinach in a neat pile in the centre of the plates.
- Arrange crumbled feta around the edge of the spinach and tomatoes to garnish.
- Thickly sprinkle almonds around the edge and add the ground pepper and salt.
- Serve with extra virgin olive oil to drizzle and lemon quarters.
  A good country bread goes well.

Spinach, Mashed Potato and Poached Eggs
Serves 2

This is my favourite dish if I am under the weather and have a fever – good too as a light supper dish.

- Prepare 450g/1lb spinach and cook, removing all water and add a little butter, salt, pepper and grated nutmeg.
- Peel, cook, mash Maris Piper potatoes - make soft and creamy.
- Place a neat pile of potatoes on a plate, top with spinach, and arrange 2 poached eggs on top.
- For a supper dish, mask with a creamy cheese sauce.

Spinach or Chard Tian
Serves 6

450g/1lb spinach
400g/ 3/4 lb new potatoes (pre-cooked)
10 anchovy fillets (cut in half)
6-7 eggs (lightly beaten)
Freshly milled black pepper, grated nutmeg
7 globe artichoke pieces (roasted in oil) – optional
4 tablespoons grated cheese (parmesan, cheddar or gruyere)

Use an oil and earthenware rectangular oven-proof dish.
- Cut the potatoes into cubes and sauté in olive oil with 2 cloves of crushed garlic for 5 minutes until golden.
- If using chard, separate the green from the stems and snip into the dish with scissors. Stalks can be used too. (Spinach should be wilted, squeezed dry and chopped).
- Add the eggs, seasonings and anchovies and grated cheese.
- Pour a little oil over the mixture and bake in a moderate oven for about 30 minutes.

Erika's Spinach with Prawns and Coconut Cream
Serves 4

280g/ ³/₄lb large peeled king prawns
450g/1lb young spinach leaves (chopped)
1 inch fresh ginger, peeled and chopped
1 lime, zest and juice
1 tablespoon palm sugar or soft brown sugar
Three-quarters red chilli, de-seeded and finely chopped
1 teaspoon sea salt
1 clove of garlic chopped
4 spring onions chopped (white parts)
1 stem lemon grass, well peeled and chopped
1 tin coconut milk
2 packets coconut cream

- Gently fry the lemon grass, ginger, chilli and spring onions and garlic in 1 tablespoon olive oil until golden.
- Add the sugar, lime juice and salt and stir well. Stir in three-quarters tin coconut milk and 1 packet coconut cream. When hot add the spinach leaves and stir until wilted.
- Add the other packet of coconut cream and the prawns, heating through.
- Cook some 'fragrant' Thai rice according to instructions.
- When cooked grease a teacup or dariole mould and press the rice firmly using a spoon.
- Turn out in the centre of a plate and spoon the spinach, prawns and coconut around.

This is also delicious cold.

GARDENING TIPS FOR SPINACH AND CHARD

SUMMER SPINACH
Likes fertile soil and plenty of water. Plant March – July in large containers with plenty of compost. The young leaves are excellent in salads. Pick constantly and try not to allow to go to seed.

SWISS CHARD
with its thick white central stem is the tastiest of the chards. The stems can be served with melted butter. Same conditions as for spinach.

RUBY CHARD
is very decorative in small containers with its red stems. Choose a selection of different colours.

STRAWBERRIES

THE STRAWBERRY IS A FRUIT OF VENUS

Strawberry and Cucumber Salad

Strawberries (all the same size)
Cucumber
Sour cream
Mint

Peel cucumber and slice thinly. Hull the strawberries and slice top to bottom. Arrange alternate layers of cucumber and strawberry on a flat serving plate. Carefully spoon sour cream over and sprinkle with chopped mint. This is particularly good with cold poached salmon and new potatoes.

Red, Red Salad

Chop everything very small
and serve as a starter.
6 large washed radishes
6 small cooked beetroot
Half a red onion
8 small tomatoes
1 small de-seeded red pepper or sweet pepper
8 medium firm strawberries
Pomegranate seeds

Dress with 4 teaspoons medium olive oil,
1 tablespoon cider vinegar, 2 teaspoons soya sauce,
1 level teaspoon whole grain mustard, salt
and pepper, and herbs such as soft thyme. Serve chilled.

Erika's Strawberry Red Kissel (Serves 6-8)

I lived in Norway and learned that most fruits can be made into Kissel, even apples. When fruit is in short supply it will increase the dish and give it volume. Frozen or bottled fruit can be used, but the strawberries must be fresh.

1 jar of stoned morello cherries
2 packs raspberries (fresh or frozen)
300g/10 $^1/_2$ oz cranberries (fresh or frozen)
2 packs fresh strawberries
50g/2oz caster sugar
1$^1/_2$ tablespoons potato flour (from health food shops)

- Put 2 cups water in a saucepan, add sugar and boil.
- Add the cranberries and wait for them to pop holding a saucepan lid in the air over them to protect them jumping.
- Add the rest of the ingredients except the strawberries and simmer gently.
- Add the sliced strawberries and cook very gently.
- Mix in the potato flour which has had a few spoonfuls of water added. It will thicken very quickly, and care must be taken for it not to go lumpy.
- Tip it into a glass bowl and sprinkle all over the surface with caster sugar.
- This is a Norwegian tip to prevent a skin from forming.
- There will be a powerful aroma of strawberries.

THIS IS A MARVELLOUS COLOURFUL DISH TO SERVE AT CHRISTMAS TIME WITH CREAM, ICE-CREAM OR MERINGUES.

FUN IDEAS WITH STRAWBERRIES

Chocolate Dipped Strawberries

THIS IS A GREAT IDEA FOR PARTIES - A DESSERT AFTERTHOUGHT, A SWEET TEMPTATION AND A LITTLE INDULGENCE.

Fresh strawberries, medium sized, firm
and a good shape.
Dark chocolate (70% cocoa mass)
White chocolate

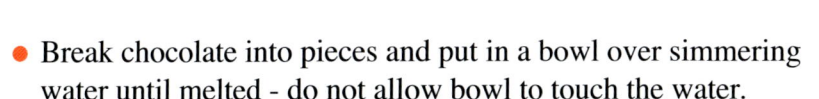

- Break chocolate into pieces and put in a bowl over simmering water until melted - do not allow bowl to touch the water.
- Cover a swiss roll tin with baking parchment.
- Dip the tip of a strawberry in the hot chocolate, spearing with a bamboo kebab stick or holding with kitchen tongs.
- Lay on the parchment and leave to harden.
- Arrange on a plate decorated with strawberry leaves.

Strawberry Souffle Omelette (serves 2)

THIS DESSERT IS A LOVELY SURPRISE AND A SOPHISTICATED TREAT. ONE MUST BE WELL ORGANISED WITH EVERYTHING READY AND YOU WILL FIND IT VERY EASY TO ACHIEVE!

2 eggs (separated) plus one extra egg white
1 1/2 tablespoons caster sugar
A few drops of pure vanilla essence
Icing sugar to sprinkle
8 strawberries
1 1/2 tablespoons home made strawberry jam
1 tablespoon butter

- Hull and cut strawberries into tiny pieces, put in a small bowl. Just before serving, mix in the strawberry jam.
- Turn the grill on to a high setting.
- Whisk egg whites until stiff, then whisk egg yolks until thick.
- Add the sugar and continue whisking until thick.
- With a metal spoon, fold in the egg whites.
- Heat the butter in a frying pan and when beginning to brown, tip in the omelette mixture.
- Cook for a few minutes, then put the pan under the grill for a few minutes - the surface should be lightly brown.
- Slide onto a serving plate and spoon strawberries onto omelette.
- Fold carefully in half and sprinkle with icing sugar.
- Make a criss cross pattern with skewers heated on the gas or under the grill - if this is too difficult, simply sprinkle with caster sugar and serve, cutting in half for two portions.
  NOTE: Mixing the strawberries with strawberry jam is a speedy option, alternatively they can be mixed with strawberry coulis. When you are familiar with the process, the omelette could be flambed with either rum or cognac.

Strawberry Marshmallow (serves 4-6)

700g/1½lbs strawberries
40g/1½ oz caster sugar
1 lemon
300ml/10fl oz/ ½ pint double cream (whipped)
15g/ ½ oz powdered gelatine
75g/3oz chopped white marshmallows
75g/3oz chopped pink marshmallows
2 egg whites (stiffly beaten)

- Pick out 6-8 small pointed strawberries for decoration.
- Slice the rest and put in a large bowl.
- Sprinkle with caster sugar and the juice of the lemon and leave for an hour.
- Dissolve the gelatine with a few spoonfuls of water in a cup in a saucepan of boiling water.
- Add to the strawberries together with the cream.
- Fold in the white marshmallows and egg whites.
- Spoon into a glass dish or small glasses.
- Decorate with strawberries and pink marshmallows.

Strawberry and Rhubarb Crumble (serves 6)

900g/2lbs pink forced rhubarb
225g/8oz strawberries
1 1/2 tablespoons golden granulated sugar
2 tablespoons flaked almonds

ALMOND CRUMBLE TOPPING
See William Pear crumble

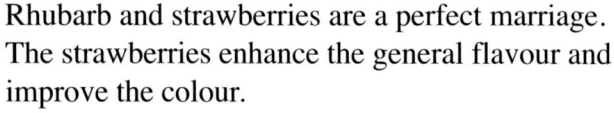

Rhubarb and strawberries are a perfect marriage. The strawberries enhance the general flavour and improve the colour.

- Snip the rhubarb into 1 inch lengths with kitchen scissors and put into a greased ovenproof dish.
- Slice the strawberries and put on top of the rhubarb, gently folding in the sugar.
- Spoon the crumble mixture carefully over the top.
- Bake for about 40 minutes in a moderate oven.
- When nearly cooked and golden, sprinkle the flaked almonds over the top with a further tablespoon of sugar.

Wild Strawberry

Coer a la Creme with Wild Strawberries (Serves 6)

Wild strawberries are hard to come by, so it is best to grow some of your own. These wonderfully fragrant little fruits are perfect for decorating the heart shaped Coeur a la Crème.

- Line heart-shaped moulds(with holes in) with fine muslin. Rub 225g/8oz cream or cottage cheese through a sieve and mix with 300ml/10fl oz/ 1/2 pint double cream and 1 1/2 dessert spoons of caster sugar.
- Fold in 2 stiffly beaten egg whites and spoon into heart moulds. Leave in the fridge overnight.
- Before serving unmould onto a plate, pour 150ml/5fl oz/ 1/4 pint single cream over and decorate with wild strawberries and a strawberry leaf on the side.

Erika's Chocolate and Strawberry Cheesecake

175g/6oz chocolate digestive biscuits (finely crushed)
400g/14oz full fat soft cheese
75g/3oz soft butter
1 tablespoon cocoa powder
100g/3 1/2 oz caster sugar
225g/8oz strawberries (liquidised and sieved)
2 level tablespoons powdered gelatine
2 eggs (separated)
300ml/10fl oz/ 1/2 pint double cream
To decorate: grated dark chocolate and sliced strawberries

- Crumb the biscuits in a food processor or bash with a hammer in a plastic bag.
- Combine with melted butter and cocoa powder.
- Line the base of a 22cm/8 inch spring release cake tin with bakewell paper.
- Press the crumbs into the tin and push a little way up the sides. Chill in the fridge for 30 minutes.
- Beat together the cheese, sugar, egg yolks and strawberry puree together in a bowl.
- Dissolve the gelatine in 4 tablespoons water in a mug placed in a pan of simmering water. Cool slightly then add to the mixture together with softly whipped cream.
- Finally, whisk the egg whites until stiff and fold into the strawberry cheese.
- Spoon into the cake tin and refrigerate overnight.
- To serve, turn out onto a plate and finely grate about 3 squares chocolate over the surface (this should be 70% cocoa solids). Arrange strawberry slices around the edge of the cheesecake, pointed ends facing outwards. Serve chilled.
Note: if a stronger strawberry flavour is desired, cut down on the double cream and add more strawberry puree.

Strawberry and Orange Jelly (Serves 4)

THIS IS A FRESH AND FRUITY-TASTING JELLY WHICH IS EASY TO MAKE AND GOOD FOR CHILDREN TOO.

1lb strawberries (hulled)
Juice of 1 1/2 oranges
Thinly pared rind of 1/2 orange
2 tablespoons caster sugar
1 packet powdered gelatine
A little double cream

- Liquidise strawberries and press through a sieve to get rid of the pips. In a bowl mix together the puree, sugar and orange juice.
- Mix the gelatine and 2 tablespoons water in a mug and put in a small saucepan of simmering water until melted.
- Add to the strawberry mixture stirring well.
- Pour into water-rinsed jelly moulds or individual glasses.
- Put the strips of orange peel in a little water with a spoonful of caster sugar. Boil until tender and the liquid syrupy.
- Remove the peel and cut into neat thin strips.
- Gently whip some double cream until nearly stiff.
- Turn out the jellies and put a spoonful of cream beside each one.
- Decorate the cream with the orange peel and a few tiny pieces of chopped strawberry.

Strawberry Chocolate Gateau for Lyn (Serves 8)

The sponge
6 eggs
Juice and rind of 1 lemon
125g/4 1/2 oz plain flour
40g/1 1/2 oz cornflour
1 teaspoon baking powder
215g/7 1/2 oz icing sugar

The icing
225g/8oz dark chocolate (70%)
125g/4 1/2 oz unsalted butter
4 egg yolks

The filling
450g/1lb strawberries
Extra strawberries
50g/2oz caster sugar
40g/1 1/2 oz gelatine
300ml/10fl oz/ 1/2 pint double cream

- Grease and line a 25-30cm (10-12 inch) tin.
- Beat egg yolks together with grated lemon rind, lemon juice and sifted sugar until thick and fluffy. Beat egg whites until stiff.
- Sift flours and baking powder.
- Carefully mix yolks and whites into flour.
- Spoon into tin and bake for 30 minutes or more until well risen and firm at 180C/350F/Gas 4.
- Turn cake onto wire rack and carefully peel off the paper.
- When cold cut into 3.
- Reserve some strawberries for dipping.
- Liquidise the rest with caster sugar.
- Dissolve the gelatine in 2 tablespoons water in a cup and heat in a pan of boiling water.
- Add to the strawberry puree together with softly whipped cream and put in fridge until almost set.
- Gently spread over cake layers, together with sliced strawberries and sandwich together.
- Melt the chocolate in a bowl over hot water, dip the tips of reserved strawberries in and place on a baking parchment to dry.

- Add butter cut in to small pieces bit by bit, beating well.
- Add yolks one by one, stirring until thick and spread quickly over the cake.
- Place chocolate strawberries in position in central circle. If liked, small strawberry leaves brushed with egg white and dipped in caster sugar (and dried in the oven) can be inserted at various intervals.

Erika's Lovely Strawberry Ice-Cream (Serves 6-8)

Most strawberry ice-creams taste as if they have been made with strawberry jam or cooked strawberry puree. This one is fresh tasting and very 'strawberryfied'!

1kg/2lbs strawberries (washed and hulled)
Juice of half a lemon
Icing sugar to taste
300ml/10fl oz double cream (softly whipped)
1 tub crème fraiche

- Liquidise the strawberries together with the lemon juice and icing sugar.
- Mix with crème fraiche and cream.
- Freeze or use an ice-cream maker.
- Decorate with fresh strawberries and leaves.

'STRAWBERRIES AND CREAM ARE CHARMING AND SWEET, MIX THEM AND TRY HOW DELIGHTFUL THEY EAT'

Old London Street Cry

Strawberry Tempura

100g/3 ½ oz self-raising flour
200ml/7fl oz sparkling mineral water
1 tablespoon rosewater
200g/7oz hulled and halved strawberries
Icing sugar to dust

- Whisk together flour, sparkling water and rosewater.
- Dip the halved strawberries into the batter, shaking off any excess.
- Shallow fry in hot vegetable oil for 2-3 minutes on each side until golden.
- Drain on kitchen paper and sprinkle with icing sugar.
- Serve with mascarpone mixed with rosewater and icing sugar and, if liked, ground cinnamon.

Dried Strawberry Slices

225g/8oz firm ripe strawberries
40g/1½ oz caster sugar

- Hull the strawberries and thinly slice lengthways.
- Carefully arrange a layer in a bowl, sprinkle with sugar and repeat until all are used.
- Pre-heat oven to 110C/225F/Gas ¼ (You may have to experiment with oven temperatures).
- With great care, lay the slices on some baking parchment on a baking sheet.
- Cook for 1½ hours, then turn slices over onto a new clean sheet of baking parchment and cook for a further hour until absolutely dry. Cool.
They can be stored in an airtight container for up to four weeks.

THESE LITTLE SLICES LOOK VERY PRETTY AND ARE USEFUL FOR DECORATING AND GARNISHING. THEY LOOK GOOD IN A CIRCLE AROUND A SCOOP OF ICE CREAM AND CAN ALSO LOOK CHARMING ON CUPCAKES OR A CLOTTED CREAM SCONE WITH STRAWBERRY JAM.

Strawberry Coulis

900g/2lbs strawberries
175g/6oz icing sugar or caster sugar
Juice of 1 lemon

- Pick over and hull the strawberries.
- Liquidise in a blender.
- Strain through a sieve to remove any 'pips'.
- Add lemon juice and sugar and stir until dissolved.
- Pour into small containers and freeze until required.

Excellent with ice-cream or a sauce for desserts.

STRAWBERRIES ARE ENGLISH SUMMERTIME AND WIMBLEDON. EVERYONE WAITS FOR THE FRAGRANT AROMA OF OUR ENGLISH GROWN STRAWBERRIES. TRY SMELLING THE HOLES IN THE PLASTIC BOXES AND ONLY BUY IF THEY SMELL OF STRAWBERRIES!

GARDENING TIPS FOR WILD STRAWBERRIES

Use either Wild or Baron Solemacher or Alexandra. They can be grown in large pots or tubs filled with compost, manure and leaf mould. They should be fed and well watered and prefer light shade. Any trailing 'suckers' should be planted in a small pot and not cut adrift until they are well rooted.

FRENCH TARRAGON

Tarragon Butter

225g/8oz butter
3 tablespoons chopped tarragon
Sea salt, freshly ground
black pepper
Juice of half a lemon

- Mix tarragon, lemon and seasoning into softened butter.
- Using cling film, shape into a sausage.
- Chill in the fridge.
- Serve with grilled steak or fish cut in rounds.

Erika's Roast Tarragon Chicken

1kg/2lb plump free-range chicken, preferably 'corn fed'
Tarragon sprigs
Soft butter to smear
500ml/18 fl oz chicken stock or white wine
1 lemon
1-2 chicken livers if possible

- Pre-heat the oven.
- Push tarragon leaves under the skin of the chicken with the help of a sharp pointed knife.
- Make a small cut and push the tarragon up the slit.
- Put the bird in a roasting dish, smear all over with soft butter.
- Sprinkle with salt and freshly ground black pepper.
- Push some tarragon and butter, the chicken liver and half a lemon inside the chicken's cavity.
- Roast for approximately 1 hour, 50 minutes at 200C/400F/Gas 6 until the skin is brown and crispy, squeezing lemon juice over the surface.
- Remove and put on a platter.
- Take the liver out and mash.
- De-glaze the pan with chicken stock or white wine, adding seasoning and the mashed liver.
- Thicken with butter and flour mixed together, adding it bit by bit.
  Serve the gravy in a jug.

Tarragon Vinegar

500ml/18fl oz white wine vinegar
Tarragon leaves

- Combine tarragon and vinegar in a plastic lidded jar.
- Leave in a sunny place, shaking from time to time.
- Strain the vinegar and use new tarragon leaves leaving for 2 weeks.
- Strain into bottles.

I sometimes put the vinegar into small plastic lidded jars with sprigs of tarragon. Use this for making Bearnaise sauce in winter-time.

Tomato and Tarragon Salsa

10 plum or medium ripe vine tomatoes (skinned and chopped)
2 spring onions, finely chopped
1 crushed garlic clove
2-3 tablespoons chopped tarragon leaves
1 teaspoon caster sugar
3 tablespoons olive oil
1 tablespoon balsamic or tarragon vinegar
Seasoning

- Make a dressing with oil, vinegar, sugar, seasoning and chopped tarragon.
- Mix in the tomatoes and tarragon and leave for a few hours for the flavours to amalgamate.
- Decorate with extra whole tarragon leaves.

Sauce Bearnaise

This is one of the most delicious sauces and can be served with steak or fish such as sole or turbot.

Several sprigs of tarragon
2 finely chopped shallots
3 tablespoons white wine vinegar or tarragon vinegar
2 tablespoons water
6 crushed black peppercorns
2 egg yolks
125g/4 $1/2$ oz butter
Salt and pepper
1 tablespoon finely chopped tarragon

- Boil the tarragon, shallots, vinegar, water and peppercorns until reduced to $1^{1}/2$ tablespoons.
- Strain and cool.
- Cream the butter and whisk the egg yolks with the cold liquid.
- Gradually add the butter a teaspoon at a time and cook carefully in a saucepan over simmering hot water.
- Add the chopped tarragon leaves.

Chicken Liver and Tarragon Spaghetti

250g/9oz spaghetti (fresh or dried)
175g/6oz fresh chicken livers
50g/1¾ oz butter
2-3 tablespoons chopped tarragon
Sea salt, freshly ground black pepper
2 shallots, peeled and finely diced
75g/3oz freshly grated parmesan
1 lemon – juice and grated rind

- Cook spaghetti according to instructions and drain.
- Fry chopped livers in brown butter together with shallots.
- Add seasoning, lemon rind and juice and tarragon.
- Tip onto the pasta and mix.

Serve with extra tarragon and grated parmesan.

Erika's Cold Tarragon Chicken (Serves 10-15)

10 chicken breasts (skinned)
1-1$^{1}/_{2}$ litres/2 pints fresh chicken stock
Bunch of tarragon sprigs
1 lemon
Salt, freshly ground black pepper
3-4 egg yolks
Beurre manie (flour and butter mixed)
Extra tarragon

- Poach the chicken breasts in the stock with lemon juice, tarragon and seasoning. A wok is good for this. Remove the breasts, cutting some in half lengthways if liked.
- Arrange on a serving platter.
- Reduce the cooking liquid by a quarter.
- Remove the tarragon sprigs.
- Add a tablespoon of finely chopped tarragon leaves and thicken with butter mixed with flour a little at a time.
- Add egg yolks one by one not heating too much.
- Carefully spoon the sauce over the chicken breasts.
- Decorate each with a single tarragon leaf.
- Garnish the platter with a few tarragon sprigs.
  Serve with a mixed green salad and baby new potatoes.

Erika's Tarragon Egg Mousse

10 hard boiled eggs, shelled and chopped
One sachet powdered gelatine
300ml/10fl oz/ 1/2 pint mayonnaise
300ml/10fl oz/ 1/2 pint double cream
1 1/2 tablespoons chopped tarragon leaves
295g tin beef consommé (condensed soup)
Seasoning and a squeeze of lemon
Webb's Wonder lettuce heart

- Heat the consommé in a saucepan according to tin instructions and add the gelatine, stirring until dissolved.
- Add a squeeze of lemon.
- Rinse a soufflé dish with cold water. Pour a little consommé in the base, arrange a few tarragon leaves around the circumference and put in the fridge to set.
- Mix the eggs, mayonnaise, whipped cream, chopped tarragon and the rest of the gelatine/consommé together.
- Take the soufflé dish out of the fridge and paint the sides with water using a pastry brush. Spoon the egg mixture into the dish and put back in the fridge to set.
- Run a knife around the mousse and place in hot water for a few seconds.
- Turn out onto a serving platter.
- Surround with finely shredded crispy Webb's Wonder heart.

*For vegetarians, use 3 tablespoons vegetable stock and vegetarian gelling agent such as agar agar, carageen or 'Vege-Gel' (made by Supercook), and a squeeze of lemon juice.

GARDENING TIPS FOR FRENCH TARRAGON

French Tarragon is the best to grow, although there are other tarragons which are not as flavoursome.
Tarragon requires a well-drained soil and a sunny, sheltered position. Fill a medium sized pot with crocks and add garden soil mixed with a little grit for drainage. Cuttings can be taken in July/August by root division, or by gently pulling a stem away from the main branch leaving a 'heel'. Dip this in hormone rooting powder and plant in small pots. A winter protection of sand is generally required around the base of the plants, although my Tarragon plant seems tough and has survived severe winters in a sheltered spot with no protection and has happily shooted in the spring!

They can be forced in winter by cutting the stems back, planting in a pot with ordinary soil and grown in a warm greenhouse, or in the home on a sunny window ledge.

TARRAGON IS INCLUDED IN DIJON MUSTARD AND SAUCE BEARNAISE.

TOMATO

'THERE IS NO SINCERER LOVE THAN THE LOVE OF FOOD'
George Bernard Shaw 1856-1950

THE TOMATO WAS ORIGINALLY A NATIVE PLANT OF SOUTH AMERICA AND WAS BROUGHT TO EUROPE BY THE SPANISH EXPLORERS. THE BRIGHT YELLOW TOMATO WAS 'THE LOVE APPLE' AND REPUTEDLY HAD APHRODISIAC QUALITIES. THEY ORIGINALLY LOOKED SIMILAR TO CHERRY TOMATOES. TOMATOES CONTAIN LYCOPENE WHICH PROTECTS AGAINST CANCER. THIS IS ONLY FOUND IN HIGH QUANTITIES IN COOKED TOMATOES – EVEN TOMATO KETCHUP.

Erika's Creamy Tomato and Parmesan Crumble
Serves 3

4-5 medium vine tomatoes
2 cloves of garlic (chopped fine)
3 medium peeled shallots (chopped)
2 tablespoons chopped parsley
175g/6oz plain flour
85g/3oz butter
25g/1oz grated parmesan cheese
2-3 tablespoons double cream
Salt and pepper
Olive oil
Fresh thyme leaves

- Slice the tomatoes in 3 or 4 and lay in a rustic oven-proof dish. Arrange the garlic, shallots, parsley and seasoning on top of each slice and drizzle sparingly with olive oil.
- Bake in a pre-heated medium oven for 40-45 minutes.
- Remove for a few minutes.
- Make a crumble with 175g/6oz plain flour and 85g/3oz butter, rubbing to crumbs.
- Add 25g/1oz grated parmesan cheese, some thyme leaves and seasoning.
- Add 2-3 tablespoons double cream to the tomatoes.
- Cover with the savoury crumble mixture and return to the oven.
- Bake for 25 minutes.
- Allow to rest for 5 minutes

Erika's Special Gazpacho (luxury version)
Serves 4-6

475g/1½lbs ripe vine tomatoes (skinned)
2 slices white bread (no crusts)
2 hard boiled egg yolks
600ml/20fl oz/1 pint fresh beef or chicken stock
Or 1 tin beef consommé
Salt, dash Tobasco sauce
2 tablespoons lime juice
1½ tablespoons extra virgin olive oil
Water, ice-cubes
Half a diced cucumber (partially peeled)
1 diced red pepper (de-seeded)
Croutons
2 peeled garlic cloves

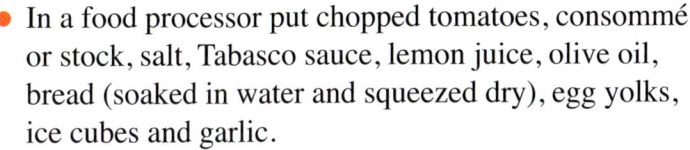

- In a food processor put chopped tomatoes, consommé or stock, salt, Tabasco sauce, lemon juice, olive oil, bread (soaked in water and squeezed dry), egg yolks, ice cubes and garlic.
- Whizz everything together. Check the seasoning and add cold water as desired.
- Serve in bowls with extra ice-cubes and diced croutons, diced peppers and cucumbers in little dishes to add to the soup.

Tomato Salsa
Serves 4

3 large vine tomatoes (peeled, seeded and diced)
1 large red bell pepper (grilled, seeded and diced)
1 large firm avocado (peeled and diced)
2 shallots (peeled and diced)
75g/2 ¾ oz sundried tomatoes (chopped small)
1 green chilli pepper (de-seeded and cut very small)
2 sweetcorn (husks and silks removed)
2 tablespoons torn basil or chopped coriander
2 tablespoons olive oil
1 lime (juice)
Salt

- Combine everything in a bowl.
- Cut the corn off the cobs.
- Dry fry the kernels in a heavy frying pan until cooked and smokey and mix with other ingredients.
- Serve in a rustic bowl sprinkled with extra herbs.
- Serve as an accompaniment to grilled steaks, chops or fish.

Erika's Tomato Summer Pudding (Serves 4)

This is suitable for a light lunch, snack or supper dish.

4-5 large ripe vine tomatoes
Fresh white bread
2 spring onions (trimmed)
Basil, caster sugar, salt
A dash of tomato puree
Webbs wonder lettuce and some rocket
4-5 hard boiled eggs

- Skin the tomatoes after immersing in boiling water.
- Cut into small chunks and reserve in a bowl.
- Line a small pudding basin with bread (crusts removed).
- Fill with tomatoes, giving a sprinkle of sugar and salt.
- Add the finely sliced spring onions and some shredded basil.
- Place a slice of bread to cover the top and press down - any bread showing above the surface of the bowl should be snipped off with kitchen scissors.
- Any left over tomato pieces can be liquidised with tomato puree and spooned over the bread.
- Turn out the tomato summer pudding onto a suitably attractive dish and surround with shredded lettuce and rocket, then arrange quarters of hard boiled egg around the dish.
- Garnish with basil leaves and dress with a vinaigrette made with dijon mustard, olive oil, red wine vinegar, salt and freshly-ground black pepper.

LIFE WITHOUT TOMATOES OR LEMONS IS LIKE LIFE WITHOUT SALT OR A GLASS OF WINE! THE FANTASTIC SMELL OF GARDEN RIPE TOMATOES IS AS TANTALISING AS COFFEE OR FRIED BACON.

TOMATOES ARE THE MOST INDISPENSABLE VERSATILE AND USEFUL FRUIT. HOW COULD WE POSSIBLY MANAGE WITHOUT THEM?? THEY FEATURE IN SAUCES, STEWS, PASTA AND SOUPS, AND ARE THE STARS OF SALSAS AND SALADS.

TOMATOES ARE ALSO PACKED WITH VITAMINS AND ARE BENEFICIAL TO ONE'S HEALTH.

Fried Green Tomatoes

Cut under ripe green tomatoes in slices. Dip in a mixture of parmesan and cornmeal. Fry until golden and crisp in hot olive oil. Serve on toast or with rosti and grilled bacon.

Erika's Tomato Haddock/Turkey Breast

- Gently fry 1 chopped shallot and 1 clove of crushed garlic until soft in 1 tablespoon olive oil.
- Add 450g/1lb skinned tomatoes, seasoning, juice of half a lemon and 1 chopped de-seeded red pepper.
- Simmer until soft.
- Add haddock pieces (or other firm fish such as monkfish or cod) and poach in the tomato sauce, turning gently.
- Serve with finely chopped parsley, a few capers and crushed new potatoes to which 1 tablespoon olive oil has been added.

A pan-fried turkey breast slice can have the same treatment. This is very good for those on a diet.

Tomato Notes

- For tomato coulis, the tomatoes should be skinned
- Plum tomatoes are best for sauces and stews
- Only use tomatoes that are deep red and smell ripe and tomatoey

Stuffed Tomatoes

Hollow out tomato halves, turn upside down to drain.

Fill with

A) Tuna, mayonnaise and capers

B) Seafood salad

C) Prawns in Marie Rose sauce with diced avocado

D) Vegetable Macedoine (diced potatoes, carrots, turnips, peas) pre-cooked and mixed with herby mayonnaise

E) Olive oil, fried breadcrumbs, finely chopped parsley, chopped shallots and garlic. Drizzle with olive oil and bake for 45 minutes.

Tomates Farcies or French Stuffed Tomatoes
(serves 6-8)

THIS IS A SIMPLE, CHEAP AND TASTY TOMATO RECIPE AND ONE CAN FIND IT IN MOST OF THE CHARCUTERIE SHOPS IN FRANCE. IT IS COUNTRY STYLE AND ECONOMICAL - THE FRENCH EAT THEM ON THEIR OWN BUT WE WOULD PROBABLY PREFER THEM SERVED WITH SAUTE OR MASHED POTATOES AND A SIMPLE GREEN SALAD.

6-8 largish vine tomatoes
450g/1lb best beef or steak mince
2 slices bread
1 egg
1 clove of garlic - crushed
2 shallots - finely chopped
2 tablespoons finely chopped parsley
Salt and freshly milled black pepper
Milk

- Cut the tomatoes near the top, leaving a slice as a 'hat'.
- Carefully cut out all the tomato flesh and leave the shells upside down to drain.
- Soak the bread in some milk, then squeeze dry so that it crumbles.
- In a bowl, combine the beef, breadcrumbs, egg, garlic, shallots, parsley, seasoning and a little milk and mix well.
- Stuff the tomatoes with the beef mixture, pressing down firmly.
- Put the 'hat' on top and arrange closely side by side in a terracotta baking dish. Lightly drizzle with olive oil and bake in a pre-heated oven 180C/350F/Gas 4 for 45 - 60 minutes.

Erika's Tomato Eggs (serves 3)

3 large eggs
3 egg yolks
4 large vine tomatoes
50g/1¾ oz butter
Salt and white pepper
Butter and toast fingers to serve

- Skin the tomatoes and chop small.
- In a non-stick frying pan, add the butter and chopped tomatoes.
- Cook gently until it had reduced considerably.
- Add all the eggs together as well as the seasoning.
- Stir gently until creamy, then take the frying pan off the stove as the eggs will continue to cook.
- Serve in little dishes with the toast fingers on the side. If liked, a few snipped chives can be sprinkled on top.

Erika's Special rustic Chicken
Serves 6

6 chicken thighs (skinned)
1 onion, peeled halved and sliced
2 x 400g tins chopped tomatoes
1 x 410g tin cannelini beans (drained)
2 cloves of garlic, peeled and chopped
2 tablespoons sherry
Chopped rosemary sprigs
75g/2 ¾ oz pitted green olives
2 small chorizo sausages – 110g/4 oz (skinned and sliced)
Olive oil
1 dessertspoon paprika, salt
3 artichoke hearts in olive oil

- Fry onions until golden in 1½ tablespoons olive oil.
- Add garlic, then chorizo - a lot of oil will emerge from the chorizo so blot it with some kitchen paper.
- Add the tomatoes, rosemary, paprika and olives.
- Cook on top of stove for 15 minutes to reduce the tomatoes.
- Add the cannelini beans and tip into a rustic terracotta oven-proof dish.
- Meanwhile fry the chicken thighs in hot olive oil and brown on both sides.
- Place in the casserole with half an artichoke under each one. (This can all be prepared a day in advance.)
- Bake in a moderately hot oven for 40 minutes.
- Serve with new potatoes.

CHICKEN THIGHS ARE CHEAPER WITH SKIN LEFT ON, LEAVING YOU TO SKIN THEM. THIS IS AN EXCELLENT FAMILY DISH. IF DESIRED, MORE CHICKEN THIGHS AND ARTICHOKES CAN BE ADDED.

Erika's Extra Special Tart for Andy
Serves 6

THIS IS ABSOLUTELY DELICIOUS FOR A LIGHT LUNCH OR SUPPER DISH, OR JUST A TASTY SNACK.

A pack of 'on the vine' cherry tomatoes
375g/13oz puff ready-rolled pastry sheet
Freshly made basil pesto
Sliced mozzarella cheese
Pine nuts
Salt, freshly ground black pepper

- Pre-heat the oven to 220C/425F/Gas 7.
- Line swiss roll tins with baking parchment.
- Unroll the pastry to approx 30cm/12 inches in length and place on top of the parchment.
- Cut in half.
- Lay 1 or 2 slices of mozzarella on top.
- Turn the pastry edges gently inwards holding the cheese in place.
- Spread the pesto generously on the cheese.
- Cut the vine tomatoes in half and neatly cover the cheese, cut side up.
- Brush tomatoes lightly with olive oil and sprinkle with salt and pepper and bake for 20 minutes.
- Remove from oven and sprinkle sparingly with pine nuts.
- Return to the oven for 5 minutes more to tint the pine nuts.
- Repeat the process on other baking trays. This should make 6 portions.

Erika's Bloody Mary Granita

Good as a tiny starter, or to refresh the palate between courses.

5 very red vine tomatoes, peeled and de-seeded
Juice of half a lemon and 1 orange
1 teaspoon celery salt
1 tablespoon tomato puree
Shake of Tobasco sauce
Shake of Worcestershire sauce
Vodka - 1 wineglass

- Whizz everything in a food processor, taste for seasoning, adding more orange juice etc.
- Freeze overnight in a small plastic container.
- Before serving break up the crystals with a fork.
- Put in small glasses with some celery heart stems, and small spoons.

GARDENING TIPS FOR TOMATOES

Tomato seedlings are ideal for garden pots and window boxes and need to be well watered and fed weekly. Liquid seaweed is good.
They should be supported by stakes, tied up with garden string and placed in a sunny site.
Tomatoes grown outdoors have a superior flavour compared with commercially grown varieties.
Cherry tomatoes are the easiest. 'Gardener's Delight' has a good flavour, 'Golden Sunrise' is a late season, and 'Tornado' is a bush tomato.

VIOLET
Viola odorata

I know a bank where the wild thyme blows
Where oxlips and the nodding violet grows
Quite over canopied with luscious woodbine
With sweet musk roses and with eglantine

William Shakespeare 1564-1616

Violet Champagne

A very unusual springtime drink, and very pretty.
Of course, sparkling white wine can be used.
Put a little liqueur 'a la violette' in a
champagne glass.
Float 2 or 3 crystallized violets
(The Fromagerie tip!) – or a few real
violets, green bits removed.

Violet syrup used sparingly could be used,
but bear in mind the colour is very strong.

*see Violet Ice-Cream for colour.

Sugared Violets

This is an easier method than for crystallized violets which involves gum tragacanth (obtainable from chemists).

Violet flowers
Caster sugar
1 egg white
1 fine paintbrush

- Lightly beat the egg white.
- Using very little, paint the violet on each side with the brush, then sprinkle with the sugar. Lay on sheets of baking parchment and leave until dry and crisp in an airing cupboard, or a very low oven with the door ajar. I always leave the stalk on as they are easier to handle - these can be cut off when dry.
- Store between layers of parchment in a plastic box.
  Great to decorate cakes and desserts.

Violet Ice-cubes

Put fresh violets in an ice-cube tray, fill with water, and freeze. These look very pretty in a spring punch or wine cup – or in a simple glass of mineral water.

Violet Butter

This is a way of preserving the violets as the butter can be cut into small sections and frozen.

225g/8oz unsalted butter (softened)
Fresh violets (green parts removed)

- Smear softened butter in an elongated shape similar to the butter pack.
- Cover with fresh violet flowers.
- Add another layer of butter covering the violets.
- Repeat the process with more violets, finishing with butter.
- Chill to harden.
- Wrap in cling-film if desired.

The violet butter can be used on scones, with rice, a spring poussin, or wherever a touch of violets is required.

Violet Vinegar

Violets are so subtle in flavour that a very mild and pale vinegar should be used. Japanese rice vinegar or white wine vinegar is best.

- Put 4 handfuls of fresh violets (green parts removed) in a bottle and fill with vinegar.
- Seal top of the bottle with a screw top or cover with cling-film.
- Leave in a sunny place for 2 weeks, strain and re-bottle and keep in a dark place.

Violet Salad

- Use the hearts of young lettuce such as Little Gem and break into pieces.
- Add a few young violet leaves, violet flowers (green parts removed), salt and pepper.
- Make a dressing with 3 parts mild olive oil or corn oil, 1 part violet vinegar, 1 teaspoon honey.
- Toss gently using your hands.
- Scatter a few extra violets on each portion.

*Use white wine vinegar if no violet vinegar available.

Mini Violet Tartlets

It is possible to buy ready-made sweet pastry cases. Choose the very small and dainty size.
Whip some double cream until thick.
Put a teaspoon into the pastry case, and a spoonful of violet petal conserve in the centre.

If liked, the cream can be coloured using the method for Violet Ice-Cream, but using very little.

White Chocolate Violet Truffles

- Melt very slowly in a bowl over gently simmering water 200g/7oz best white chocolate.
- When melted add 1$^1/_2$ tablespoons violet essence and a drop of colouring*.
- Stir in 2 teaspoons runny honey, put in fridge for 30 minutes.
- Scoop the mixture with a teaspoon and roll into balls. Put some crystallized violet petals into a paper bag and bash with a hammer to crush.
- Roll the chocolate ball in the crushed petals and serve as an original treat with coffee.
- Alternatively the chocolate balls could be quickly dipped in dark melted chocolate (use a cocktail stick) and garnish with one crystallized violet.
*See Violet Ice-Cream for colouring.

THE BEAUTIFUL SCENTED PURPLE VIOLET HAS CHARMED PEOPLE FOR THOUSANDS OF YEARS. GROW A PATCH OF THEM IN YOUR GARDEN OR PLANT POT AND ENJOY THEIR LINGERING SWEET PERFUME. ADMIRE THEIR ROMANTIC HEART-SHAPED LEAVES.
USE THEM IN DELICATELY FRAGRANT RECIPES TO SURPRISE AND DELIGHT YOUR FRIENDS.
THE VIOLET HAS ALWAYS BEEN A LITERARY INSPIRATION TO POETS AND AUTHORS AND IS CONSTANTLY QUOTED. THE ROMANS PERFUMED THEIR WINE WITH THEM, AND IN 15TH CENTURY ENGLAND FLOWER AND HERB SALADS WERE CREATED. VIOLETS, PRIMROSES AND BORAGE FLOWERS WERE USED, AND SOMETIMES YOUNG VIOLET LEAVES. THEY ALSO DECORATED SALAMAGUNDY. IN VICTORIAN TIMES VIOLETS WERE SO POPULAR THAT THEY WERE GROWN IN COLD FRAMES SO THAT THEY COULD BE PICKED THROUGHOUT THE YEAR.

Violet Panecotta
Serves 6

700ml/25fl oz/1¼ pints single cream
200ml/7fl oz full fat milk
150g/5 ½ oz caster sugar
4 ½ gelatine leaves
1½ tablespoons violet essence
(Arome Violette)
A few crystallized violets and, if possible,
a violet leaf to decorate.

- Put the cream, sugar and milk in a saucepan and very slowly bring to below boiling point.
- Soften the gelatine in a little warm water.
- Squeeze excess water from the gelatine and add to the hot cream, stirring until dissolved, with a wooden spoon.
- Add the violet essence and pour into 6 dariole moulds.
- Chill overnight.
- Turn out onto pretty plates.
- Decorate with a few crystallized violets and a violet leaf.

This is very pleasant with a poached pear (William or Conference).
Should the panecotta not set properly, turn it out as a sauce and sprinkle with violets.

Erika's Violet Pavlova
Serves 6

This is a very good idea for those who do not have violet essence, syrup, jam, etc.

4 egg whites
225g/8oz caster sugar
1 teaspoon white wine vinegar
1 teaspoon cornflour
300ml/ ½ pint double cream
100g/3 ½ oz violet chocolate creams
A few crystallized violets

- Pre-heat oven to 130C/275F/Gas ½ and cover a baking tray with baking parchment.
- Whisk the egg whites until stiff and fold in the sugar, one tablespoon at a time.
- Fold in the vinegar and cornflour.
- Spoon the meringue to form a circle shape onto the baking parchment.
- Build up spoonfuls around the edge to give a little height.
- Bake for 50 minutes and after 5 minutes lower temperature to 120C/250F/Gas ¼ .
- Cool the pavlova and place on a suitable plate then whip the cream until thick.
- At the last minute before serving, spoon cream onto the pavlova.
- Chop the violet chocolate creams into small pieces and scatter over the surface together with a few crystallized violets.

Violet Cream Sponge

This is a lovely cake for special occasion or dinner party gateau.

150g/5oz plain flour, sieved with a pinch
of salt and a pinch of baking powder
225g/8oz caster sugar
4 eggs
1 dessertspoon violet essence

- Prepare an 8 inch round loose-bottomed tin by greasing and sprinkling with sugar then flour.
- Tip excess away and set oven to 180C/350F/Gas4.
- Beat egg whites until stiff, beating in half the sugar.
- Beat egg yolks with rest of sugar until thick and pale, adding violet essence.
- Fold carefully into the egg whites with a metal spoon then gradually fold in the flour very gently.
- Bake for 30-35 minutes until firm, golden and well risen.
- Turn out onto a wire rack and when cool cut into 2 or 3.
- Spread one layer with violet petal conserve, the other with whipped double cream then press the layers together.
- Spread with an icing made from icing sugar, one tablespoon violet essence and a very little violet* colouring.
- Add a spoonful of water to dilute if necessary and allow to drip down the sides of the cake.
- Decorate with crystallized violets when icing is beginning to set.

*Mix violet syrup and cochineal as in Violet Ice-Cream.
Icing must be kept a delicate colour.
Alternatively mix blue food colouring and cochineal in a ramekin and use a cotton bud to drip the colour onto the icing.

Green leaves or stalks can be made from crystallized angelica.

Violet Ice-cream
Serves 6

This is an ice-cream short cut. Use a good quality
vanilla ice-cream made with cream and eggs.
Should you want to make your own, use the recipe of
ROSEY ICE-CREAM under ROSE. Omit Turkish Delight,
cochineal, and rosewater. Instead add Violet essence and
a few drops of violet colouring.

- Scoop vanilla ice-cream into a bowl.
- Add 1 tablespoon violet essence and stir.
- Mix the colour using a small ramekin dish, adding
  1 tablespoon violet syrup and 2 drops of cochineal.
- Stir thoroughly, and fold into the ice-cream.
- Replace in original container and freeze.

Serve in tiny glasses with either a fresh or crystallized violet
and a violet leaf as decorations. Please use a small coffee
spoon – this is a poetic, magical dessert of originality and charm.

*An extra idea for VIOLET ICE-CREAM
Fry some fresh brown breadcrumbs in unsalted butter until crisp.
Pat with kitchen paper to remove any excess butter.
Mix with a tablespoon demerara sugar and some lightly crushed
crystallized violets.
Serve with a scoop of violet ice-cream in the centre of a glass or
plain plate with a spoonful of crispy crumbs around the edge.

THE FROMAGERIE in LONDON stocks several violet products. These come from Toulouse, France, the centre of violet growers, and are made from natural ingredients.

Violet gastronomic goods available are:

Violet syrup (sirop a la violette)
Violet essence (Arome violette)
Violet liqueur (Liqueur a la violette)
Violet tea from Jardin d'eben Toulouse (sold loose by weight)
Crystallized violets

They have kindly agreed to mail order these products.

The Fromagerie
2-4 Moxon Street
London W1V 4EW
Telephone: 020 7935 0341
www.lafromagerie.co.uk

'Lakeland' stock Violet Petal Conserve which is made in France and has a good violet flavour. Contact them at:-

Lakeland
Alexandra Buildings
Windermere
Cumbria
LA23 1BQ
Tel:01539 488100
www.lakeland.co.uk
(They do mail-order)

GARDENING TIPS FOR VIOLETS

The violet grows in the wild and is cultivated in gardens. They prefer a rich moist soil and partial shade. Give them plenty of compost and leaf mould. They also benefit from a seaweed spray. They will be happy in flower pots which can be moved to extra shade in hot weather.

INDEX

Apples and Pears

Apple and Parsnip Soup	7
Apple and Herring	8
Apple Sauce with Quinces	8
Apple Puree with Vanilla	10
My Chicken Normande	9
Caramel Pears	10
Erika's Fantastic William Pear Trifle	13
Erika's Harvest Apple Trifle	14
Cider Syllabub	11
William Pears Stuffed with Marzipan	11
William Pear and Almond Crumble	12

Fine Green Beans

Green Bean Banquet	19
Green Bean (Starter or Salad)	15
Green Bean and Pancetta Bundles	13
Green Bean Salsa	16
Green Green Soup	21
Beans, Bacon, Pear and Potato	17
Salad Nicoise	18
Green Beans and Flageolets	22
Fricasse of Mixed Beans with Almonds	20

Blueberry or Bilberry

Lamb Chops or Noisettes with Blueberries	23
Blueberry and Maple Cheesecake	24
Blueberry Sauce to Serve with Game	25
Erika's Blueberry and Lime Syllabub	27
Blueberry Frangipane Slice	26

Blueberry Buttermilk Pancakes with Maple Syrup	28
Blueberry and Poppy-Seed Lemon Drizzle Cake	29
Blueberry Almond Honey Cake	30

Courgettes

Courgette Coconut and Dill Soup	31
Courgette and Green Pepper Brochettes	32
Courgette Ribbons	32
Courgette and Olive Frittata	33
Little Courgette Fritters	34
Erika's Special Caponata	35
Terrine of Courgettes and Spinach with Tomato Coulis	36
Tomato and Orange Coulis	38
Mushroom Stuffed Courgettes	37
A Crumb Topping	37

Lavender

Lavender Salt	39
Lavender Sugar	40
Lavender Cream	40
Roast Lamb with Lavender	41
Erika's Lavender Honeycomb	42
Erika's Crunchy Little Lavender and Pinenut Cakes	43
Lavender Pancakes	44
Lavender Scones	44
Lavender Shortbread	44
Lavender Crème Brulee	44
Lavender Vinegar	44
Erika's Lavender and Roasted Fig Ice-Cream	45

Mint

Erika's Special Tomato, Mint and Orange Soup	46
Iced Mint and Cucumber Soup	48
Slow Roast Leg/Shoulder of Lamb with Dates and Couscous	47
Baby Vegetables with Mint	48
Pineapple with Mint	48
Erika's Pepper, Chilli and Mint Chutney	51
Home-Made Mint Tea	51
Extra Special Couscous	49
Grandmother's Herby Yorkshire Pudding	50

Peas

Iced Green Pea and Lettuce Soup	53
Mushy Pea Soup with Ham	54
Curried Pea Puree	54
Mangetout Peas with Prawns	57
French Peas with Veal or Duck	58
Grandmother's Pea Sandwiches	59
Erika's Pea Mousse with Prawns and Crispy Bacon	55
Lemon, Chilli and Pea Spaghetti	56
Pea Dip	59

Raspberries

Raspberry Alaska	62
Raspberry Jelly and Creamy Custard	61
Raspberry Hazelnut Meringue	63
Tarte Cardinale	64
Raspberry Vinegar	64
A Raspberry Summer Drink	67
Raspberry Champagne	67
Fresh Summery Raspberry Mousse	65

Lacy Raspberry Ice-cream Pancakes	65

Roses

Erika's Rosey Ice-Cream with Turkish Delight	72
White Chocolate Rose Truffles	72
Erika's Rose Summertime Sponge for Rozelle	70
Rose Petal Jam	71
Lamb Kebabs with Rose	73
Rose Vinegar	73
Rose Petal Sandwiches	71

Salad Leaves

Hazelnut Salad	78
Walnut Salad with Pears	78
Orange Salad	78
Erika's Rose Salad	79
Fig or Nectarine Salad	82
Quail's Egg Salad	80
Roasted Vegetable Salad	81

Spinach and Swiss Chard

Spinach and Smoked Haddock Soup	83
Spinach Ramekins	85
Spinach, Cottage Cheese and Pineapple	86
Spinach and Ricotta Tartlets	84
Salad of Spinach, Feta Cheese, Tomatoes and Almonds	87
Spinach, Mashed Potato and Poached Eggs	88
Spinach or Chard Tian	88
Erika's Spinach with Prawns and Coconut Cream	89

Strawberries

Strawberry and Cucumber Salad	91
Red, Red Salad	91
Erika's Strawberry Red Kissel	92
Strawberry Marshmallow	95
Strawberry and Rhubarb Crumble	96
Strawberry Coulis	105
Coeur a la Crème with Wild Strawberries	98
Strawberry Chocolate Gateau for Lyn	101
Erika's Lovely Strawberry Ice-Cream	102
Chocolate Dipped Strawberries	93
Strawberry Souffle Omelette	94
Erika's Chocolate and Strawberry Cheesecake	99
Strawberry and Orange Jelly	100

Tarragon

Tarragon Butter	107
Tarragon Vinegar	109
Tomato and Tarragon Salsa	109
Erika's Tarragon Egg Mousse	87
Chicken Liver and Tarragon spaghetti	111
Erika's Roast Tarragon Chicken	108
Erika's Cold Tarragon Chicken	112
Sauce Bearnaise	110

Tomatoes

Erika's Special Gazpacho (luxury version)	117
Erika's Special Tart for Andy	126
Tomato Salsa	118

Erika's Bloody Mary Granita	127
Fried Green Tomatoes	120
Erika's Creamy Tomato and Parmesan Crumble	116
Erika's Tomato Haddock/Turkey Breast	121
Erika's Special Rustic Chicken	125
Stuffed Tomatoes	122
Erika's Tomato Summer Pudding	119
Tomates Farcies or French Stuffed Tomatoes	123
Erika's Tomato Eggs	124

Violet

Violet Champagne	129
Sugared Violets	130
Violet Ice-Cubes	130
Violet Butter	131
Violet Vinegar	131
Violet Salad	132
White Chocolate Violet Truffles	133
Mini Violet Tartlets	132
Violet Panecotta	134
Erika's Violet Pavlova	135
Violet Cream Sponge	136
Violet Ice-Cream	137

RECIPE INDEX

Soups

Erika's Special Gazpacho (luxury version)	117
Courgette Coconut and Dill Soup	31
Apple and Parsnip Soup	7
Mushy Pea and Ham Soup	54
Spinach and Smoked Haddock Soup	83
Erika's Special Tomato, Mint and Orange Soup	46
Iced Mint and Cucumber Soup	48
Green, Green Soup	21

Starters

Erika's Bloody Mary Granita	127
Stuffed Tomatoes	122
Apple and Herring	8
Walnut Salad with Pears	78
Spinach Ramekins	85
Green Bean Starter or Salad	15
Erika's Pea Mousse with Prawns and Crispy Bacon	55
Terrine of Courgettes and Spinach with Tomato Coulis	36
Pea Dip	59

Light Lunch or Supper Dishes

Beans, Bacon, Pear and Potato	17
Courgette and Olive Frittata	33
Green Bean Banquet	19
Salad Nicoise	18

Terrine of Courgettes and Spinach with Tomato Coulis	36
Mushroom Stuffed Courgettes	37
Lemon, Chilli and Pea Spaghetti	56
Chicken Liver and Tarragon Spaghetti	111
Erika's Special Tomato Tart for Andy	126
Erika's Creamy Tomato and Parmesan Crumble	116
Stuffed Tomatoes	122

Fish

Salad Nicoise	18
Mangetout Peas with Prawns	57
Erika's Spinach with Prawns and Coconut Cream	89
Erika's Tomato Haddock or Turkey Breast	121
Stuffed Tomatoes with Tuna Mayonnaise and Capers	122
Stuffed Tomatoes with Seafood Salad	122
Stuffed Tomatoes with Prawns in Marie Rose Sauce with diced Avocado	122

Meat and Poultry

My Chicken Normande	9
Lamb Chops or Noisettes with Blueberries	23
Slow Roast Leg/shoulder of Lamb with Dates and Couscous	47
French Peas with Veal or Duck	58
Lamb Kebabs with Rose	73
Chicken Liver and Tarragon Spaghetti	111
Erika's Roast Tarragon Chicken	108
Erika's Cold Tarragon Chicken	112
Roast Lamb with Lavender	41
Erika's Tomato Haddock or Turkey Breast	121
Erika's Special Rustic Chicken	125

Vegetables

Green Bean and Pancetta Bundles	13
Green Beans and Flageolets	22
Fricasse of Mixed Beans with Almonds	20
Courgette and Olive Frittata	33
Courgette and Green Pepper Brochettes	32
Courgette Ribbons	32
Extra Special Couscous	49
Mushroom Stuffed Courgettes	37
A Crumb Topping	37
Baby Vegetables with Mint	48
Curried Pea Puree	54
French Peas with Veal or Duck	58
Fried Green Tomatoes	120
Erika's Tomato Summer Pudding	119
Erika's Creamy Tomato and Parmesan Crumble	116
Stuffed Tomatoes	122
Tomatoes Farcies or French Stuffed Tomatoes	123
Erika's Tomato Eggs	124

Desserts

Apple Puree with Vanilla	10
Blueberry and Maple Cheesecake	24
Caramel Pears	10
Erika's Harvest Apple Trifle	14
Cider Syllabub	11
William Pears stuffed with Marzipan	11
William Pear and Almond Crumble	12
Erika's Fantastic William Pear Trifle	13
Erika's Blueberry and Lime Syllabub	27
Blueberry Frangipane Slice	26
Blueberry Buttermilk Pancakes with Maple Syrup	28

Pineapple with Mint	48
Lacy Raspberry Ice-cream Pancakes	66
Raspberry Alaska	62
Fresh Summery Raspberry Mousse	65
Raspberry Jelly with Creamy Custard	61
Raspberry Hazelnut Meringue	63
Tarte Cardinale	64
Erika's Rosey Ice-Cream with Turkish Delight	72
Erika's Rose Summertime Sponge for Rozelle	70
Erika's Strawberry Red Kissel	92
Chocolate Dipped Strawberries	93
Erika's Chocolate and Strawberry Cheesecake	100
Strawberry and Orange Jelly	95
Strawberry Marshmallow	95
Strawberry Souffle Omelette	95
Strawberry and Rhubarb Crumble	96
Coeur a la Crème with Wild Strawberries	98
Strawberry Chocolate Gateau for Lyn	101
Erika's Lovely Strawberry Ice-Cream	102
Erika's Lavender Honeycomb	42
Erika's Lavender and Roasted Fig Ice-Cream	45
Mini Violet Tartlets	132
Violet Pannacotta	134
Erika's Violet Pavlova	135

Ice-cream

Erika's Raspberry Alaska	62
Erika's Rosey Ice-Cream with Turkish Delight	72
Erika's Lovely Strawberry Ice-Cream	102
Erika's Lavender and Roasted Fig Ice-Cream	45
Violet Ice-Cream	137

Salads

Quail's Egg Salad	80
Salad Nicoise	18
Hazelnut Salad	78
Walnut Salad with Pears	78
Orange Salad	78
Erika's Rose Salad	79
Fig or Nectarine Salad	82
Roasted Vegetable Salad	81
Salad of Spinach, Feta Cheese, Tomatoes and Almonds	87
Violet Salad	132

Drinks

Homemade Mint Tea	51
Raspberry Summer Drink	67
Raspberry Champagne	67
Erika's Bloody Mary Granita	127
Violet Champagne	129
Violet Ice-Cubes	130

Cakes and Gateaux

Erika's Crunchy Little Lavender and Pinenut Cakes	43
Lavender Shortbread	44
Lavender Scones	44
Violet Cream Sponge	136
Strawberry Chocolate Gateau for Lyn	101
Raspberry Scones	67
Erika's Rose Summertime Sponge for Rozelle	70
Blueberry and Poppy Seed Lemon Drizzle Cake	29
Erika's Blueberry Almond Honey Cake	30

Miscellaneous

Apple Sauce with Quinces	8
Blueberry Sauce to Serve with Game	25
Erika's Pepper, Chilli and Mint Chutney	51
Homemade Mint Tea	51
Grandmother's Pea Sandwiches	59
Grandmother's Herby Yorkshire Pudding	50
Raspberry Vinegar	64
Rose Petal Jam	71
Rose Vinegar	73
Rose Petal Sandwiches	71
Strawberry Coulis	105
Tarragon Butter	107
Tarragon Vinegar	109
Tomato and Tarragon Salsa	109
Sauce Bearnaise	110
Tomato Salsa	118
Lavender Salt	39
Lavender Sugar	40
Lavender Cream	40
Lavender Vinegar	44
Sugared Violets	130
Violet Ice Cubes	130
Violet Butter	131
Violet Vinegar	131
White Chocolate Violet Truffles	133

ERIKA PARRY

*A very big thank you to
TIM WALKER who kindly
took this photograph.

NOTES